Different Thinking

Different Thinking is the result of a special collaboration between Kogan Page and Redline Wirtschaft, Germany's leading business publisher. Selected best-selling titles previously published by Redline Wirtschaft are translated into English and published by Kogan Page to ensure a worldwide distribution.

Different Thinking

Creative strategies for developing the innovative business

Anja Foerster & Peter Kreuz

**KOGAN
PAGE**

London and Philadelphia

Publisher's note

Every possible effort has been made to ensure that the information contained in this book is accurate at the time of going to press, and the publishers and authors cannot accept responsibility for any errors or omissions, however caused. No responsibility for loss or damage occasioned to any person acting, or refraining from action, as a result of the material in this publication can be accepted by the editor, the publisher or any of the authors.

Originally published in Germany in 2005 as *Different Thinking* by Redline Wirtschaft, Redline Wirtschaft GmbH Heidelberg, Germany, a division of Süddeutcher Verlag | Mediengruppe
First published in Great Britain and the United States in 2007 by Kogan Page Limited

120 Pentonville Road
London N1 9JN
United Kingdom
www.kogan-page.co.uk

525 South 4th Street, #241
Philadelphia PA 19147
USA

ISBN-10   0 7494 4840 7
ISBN-13   978 0 7494 4840 0

British Library Cataloguing-in-Publication Data

A CIP record for this book is available from the British Library.

Library of Congress Cataloging-in-Publication Data

Fœrster, Anja.
  Different thinking : creative strategies for developing the innovative business / Anja Fœrster and Peter Kreuz.
      p. cm.
  Includes bibliographical references and index.
  ISBN-13: 978-0-7494-4840-0
  ISBN-10: 0-7494-4840-7
1. Creative ability in business. 2. Strategic planning. 3.
Organizational change. 4. Industrial management–Technological
innovations. I. Kreuz, Peter. II. Title. III. Title: Creative
strategies for developing the innovative business.
  HD53.F665 2007
  658.4'012--dc22
                                                        2007017734

Typeset by Saxon Graphics Ltd, Derby
Printed and bound in Great Britain by MPG Books Ltd, Bodmin, Cornwall

Praise for the authors

A fascinating book ...

... that provides examples and inspiration to bring the reader a step closer to those successful unconventional thinkers who change the world and a step further away from the broad mass of hangers-on who do what they have always done: nothing.

Gerhard Zakrajsek, Branch Head, IBM Austria

For all those who long to break the laws of conventional everyday business life – inspiration and ideas for innovative action to implement successful business ideas.

Katarina Loksa, Marketing Manager, Procter & Gamble, Europe

'Be different, be fast, be relevant!' – Never more important than it is today, and never has a book provided more inspiration than *Different Thinking*. An absolute must-read!

Andreas Peters, Head of Marketing, Maggi Germany

This book is just the ticket for all those who have been following the same old routine for 30 years. And for those who make a fresh start with each new challenge. And for all those who hate rigid rules. And for anyone else, too!

Paul Hysek, CEO, Management Club Vienna

... advice straight from the heart. Think unconventionally and differentiate to get that competitive edge, that's what we all aim to do with our companies. A highly recommendable book!

Ronald Renggli, Chairman of the Board, Simultan AG

Out-of-the-box thinking with practical relevance! This book encourages you to demand the exceptional from yourself and to implement exceptional ideas in everyday business life. It shows its readers how to stand out from their competitors and to react quickly to changing conditions with innovative and successful strategies.

Ingo Frank, Manager, Deloitte Consulting

An extremely motivating book for those looking for change. Using practical examples, it shows you how to stop thinking and acting along those old conventional lines and become a business unconventionalist.

Elmar Wohlgensinger, President of the GfM, Swiss Marketing Society

Different Thinking – a book that will make the business world sit up and listen! A book that shows its readers how important it is to look over the edge of their teacups and be open for new ideas.

Svenja Thimm, Management-Center Handwerk NRW

This book is a refreshing invitation to break away from old-established (thought) patterns and tread new paths. Anja Förster and Peter Kreuz are convincing pioneers of radical, cutting-edge innovation.

Dr Bruno Weisshaupt, CEO, TMG Systeminnovation AG, Frauenfeld

Contents

plummeting – and win 158; Pricing in-between. Be smart – position yourself in the middle of the market 167; The Rockefeller Principle: give away the lamp and sell the oil 174; Personalized price: let the customer set the price 177; Free price: offer freebies to your customers and let others foot the bill 184

Introduction

This book is for you!

Here's to the crazy ones, the misfits, the rebels, the troublemakers, the round pegs in the square holes. The ones who see things differently. They're not fond of rules and they have no respect for the status quo. You can quote them, disbelieve them, glorify or vilify them. About the only thing you can't do is ignore them, because they change things. They push the human race forwards. While some may see them as the crazy ones, we see genius. Because the ones who are crazy enough to think that they can change the world are the ones who do.

Advert for Apple Computer

This book was written for all those who want to make a difference – in their world and in their organization. It is a book for all those who refuse to succumb to the cynicism of a Dilbert and who are crazy enough to dare to try something new: Business unconventionality!

Our firm conviction: it is madness to keep on following the same old routines yet expect to achieve different results. Dare to be different, to question the seemingly irrefutable laws of your industry, and remember the words of German journalist, satirist and writer Kurt Tucholsky, 'Never trust an expert who tells you he's been doing things that way for 20 years. It could be he's been doing it wrong for 20 years.'

No moaning!

This is a book for anyone who has had enough of endless debates in the style of late night political talk shows, where they talk and talk but nothing ever changes. It is a book for all those who deliberately set out to counteract the trend of high-level moaning and groaning, and who are convinced of one thing: the future is something we create, not something that happens to us. It is a book for all those for whom their passionate belief in what they are doing is just as important as financial gain. It speaks to people who believe that it is time to cast conventional mindsets overboard. It is a book for all those who refuse to believe that old-established companies are not capable of being innovative. This book is intended both for those who are sick and tired of always playing on the safe side, and those who are not prepared to sacrifice their dreams on the altar of conventional wisdom.

The best way to read this book

This book is intended as a hands-on guide, so do feel free to pick out the ideas that are most useful for you from the individual chapters. But of course, we won't mind at all if you read the book from cover to cover first and then decide which ideas and concepts are of most benefit to you.

Read the book with the right fighting spirit! It is intended as a workbook. Underline relevant passages, make your own notes, turn down the corners of the most important pages and stick Post-its on the pages. Do whatever you need to do to get the most out of this book.

Run through the proposed strategies in your mind, and put them to work in your company. See the ideas as pieces of a jigsaw puzzle to be played around with as you wish. Find out how the individual pieces work, enhance them, mix and match them.

> The only sure way to avoid making mistakes is to have no new ideas!
>
> Albert Einstein

For us, the rules of business unconventionality are not indisputable truths, but tools which help companies dramatically increase productivity and earning power.

This book is a call to arms for all those who are sick and tired of running the same old procedures and process over and over again. Even if your team or your division is very successful with the old routines. The rules we present can help you and your colleagues see things from a different perspective. They can teach you to look over the rim of your teacup, to see old problems from a new vantage point and free yourself from the restraints of the past.

But – and this is a very big but

Perhaps, in the course of reading this book, you will find yourself murmuring things like 'That doesn't apply to my company,' or 'Our industry is completely different,' or 'That wouldn't work with our customers'. In many companies there is a firm belief that their own organization is so special that it cannot learn from any other organization or industry. That, of course, is simply not true, and it is precisely this way of thinking that robs people of the ability to look beyond the borders of their organization and to find new and fresh ideas elsewhere.

A manufacturer of nuts and bolts has just as much in common with a hotel as one bank with another. Everything in the world of business revolves around resources, deals and people. You want to work more efficiently? You want to be faster? You want to achieve more? Then the first thing you have to do is get rid of the ballast that is weighing you down.

'We've always done it that way.' Well, forget it! 'That won't work in my company.' Have you tried? 'We simply don't have the time to reorganize our organization.' If that is really the case, you'd better start looking for a new employer!

Different thinking

If you are determined to be smarter, more successful and to really stand out from the rest, then this is the right book for you. You can learn from the wealth of examples from the business world presented here, and find tried and tested strategies for your personal success. Are you ready?

The rules of business unconventionality at a glance

Rule 1   The 360° view: glean inspiration from other industries.

Rule 2   Dead centre: get out of those middle-of-the-market segments – fast!

Rule 3   Travel light. Cut the ballast.

Rule 4   Out of the box: create completely new markets.

Rule 5   Maxi size and mini size: place no geographical limits on your success.

Rule 6   Mix it! Conquer new markets with innovative combinations.

Rule 7   Quasi-monopolies: be the champion. Create a monopoly in your market.

Rule 8   Product DNA: question the existing product concepts.

Rule 9   Design matters: design as a competitive factor.

Rule 10   Experience inside: create an experience, trigger emotions.

Rule 11   Easy Inc: offer clarity, cut out the frills to make your product irresistible.

Rule 12   Price DNA: question the established price models.

Rule 13   Price polarization: send your prices skyrocketing or plummeting – and win!

Rule 14   Pricing in-between: be smart – position yourself in the middle of the market.

Rule 15   The Rockefeller Principle: give away the lamp and sell the oil.

Rule 16   Personalized price: let the customer set the price.

Rule 17   Free price: offer freebies to your customers and let others foot the bill.

One thing's for sure: mediocrity never wins!

We live in an age of constant change. Even the market leaders are forced to keep redefining themselves in order to defend their position on the market. If they failed to do so, they would either be caught napping by new developments and swept off the market, or copied – and in the end ousted – by ambitious rivals: today a market leader, tomorrow run-of-the-mill, the day after tomorrow doomed to insignificance.

Wealth flows directly from innovation, not optimization... wealth is not gained by perfecting the known.

Kevin Kelly, IT guru

It would be naïve simply to sit there and expect customers to come flocking to you, and to believe that your competitors won't be doing everything in their power to steal your share of the market.

We live in the age of hyper-competition, with a vast number of companies all competing for the customers' favour. And customers can pick and choose nowadays: new products and services are appearing on the market every day. Product life cycles are getting shorter and shorter, while at the same time most target groups are well supplied. Maybe you haven't realized it yet, but somewhere, one of your competitors has just had a bright idea on how to steal a slice of your cake. If you are lucky, you will notice it in time and be able to take appropriate action. If you're unlucky, you won't notice until it's too late.

So if you don't start looking for new ideas right away, you are going to lose the race!

Jonas Ridderstråle and Kjell Nordström, professors at the renowned Stockholm School of Economics, call this *Funky Business*. In their book of the same name, they make the argument that companies can only be successful if the people in them are capable of thinking differently. The future belongs to the unconventionalists, to those who dare to take risks, to break old rules and make new ones. The future belongs to those who seize the opportunity to do just that.

If we are willing to take a small risk, to break one tiny rule, to deviate just slightly from the norm, there is at least a theoretical chance that we might achieve different results, discover a niche, create a temporary monopoly and make money.

Jonas Ridderstråle and Kjell Nordström

The normal and the average are increasingly becoming symbols of mediocrity, not only of the mediocre products and services a company offers, but also of the mediocre people who work there. Just take a look around you in the airport business lounges, in offices, wherever the species of human beings we call managers congregate. Grey is the dominant colour and humour is a rarity. The corridors of our companies and the airport buildings are full of sad figures that dress and even look alike. They have wardrobes full of suits in the same dull shades of medium and dark grey with pinstripes, or medium and dark grey without pinstripes. In management circles, the willingness to be different is about as popular as the willingness to take risks, and – we presume – a character fault that is surgically removed before anyone is promoted to middle management.

And the result? Anyone who takes the same approach as everyone else and thinks in exactly the same way is bound to turn out identical products and sell them on exactly the same markets. And the customers? They punish conformity and uniformity of products and services with the toughest penalty they can impose. They simply go for the lowest price. If all products are much the same, then customers will choose the cheapest. So to be a real winner, you have to be prepared to break out.

Remember the words of the eternal neurotic Woody Allen, who once said, 'To be successful, you have to be different.' And business unconventionalists are different every time!

Business unconventionality

Business unconventionality means competing with your rivals in the fields of imagination, inspiration and initiative – and beating them. Every time, in every industry and with all the consequences. And business unconventionality is not limited to your products. It is the mindset and attitude with which you go to your office or your workbench every day, one that you don't leave behind you at the gate when you leave the premises after work. Business unconventionality means being constantly on the lookout for new ideas, smart strategies and new paths.

The magic word here is *change*. Tom Peters, American best-selling author and management guru, sums it all up:

> Individually and as companies, we have to learn to strive for change and innovation with the same fervour with which we fought them in the past.

Behaviour patterns that have worked in the past and on which the success of the company was based must not be allowed to become sacred cows. The willingness to re-examine old habits must become a matter of course. We must constantly question rules and behaviour patterns which up to now have been regarded as sacrosanct. And we must be prepared to bring about change and new development. This also means that you must be prepared to re-examine the alignment of your company every day, to be a pioneering and unconventional thinker. A large part of your work will consist of keeping an eye on the markets, tracking and picking up on trends, not just nationally, but internationally, because you don't have to reinvent the wheel every day. You can profit from ideas that have already been employed successfully elsewhere – outside your established market.

'Easier said than done,' you might think. 'But I've got the pressing day-to-day business to take care of as well.' True, and we do tend to focus on the urgent matters in hand rather than on what is really important. But we must not let our urgent day-to-day business distract us from such important considerations. Not even when business is booming!

'But isn't that exhausting?' Of course it is – but is there an alternative? We don't think so, because one thing is for certain: mediocrity never wins. Never has done and never will do!

The path to success

'We've hardly got a minute to think, let alone think unconventionally!' We often hear this and similar statements from managers. And so let's start off with the good news: We can help you! How? We can show you promising new approaches, introduce you to organizations and managers who have left the beaten paths and are following new strategies, who have upended established business conventions or discovered completely new markets.

It's not a question of slavishly copying these examples. Some brainwork on your part is required, too. But we can promise you this: you will get 100 per cent inspiration – although a little effort on your part is required as well! The strategies of business unconventionality will provide you with the tools you need to break out of the status quo and tread new ground.

In the four main sections of this book, we present four strategies that together form the basis of the concept of business unconventionality:

- Question your strategies.
- Create new markets.
- Give your products a radical makeover.
- Invent new profit models.

1 Different thinking: strategy

There are new worlds to be conquered out there.

Rupert Murdoch, media mogul

What does unconventional thinking in business have to do with strategy? A great deal! However, let us start by taking a look at what business unconventionality is *not*. It is not a code of action for managers eagerly striving to maintain the status quo, managers who dig in their heels, resist all change and place more trust in what was successful yesterday than in what will be the source of future success. We would like to illustrate this with the following story.

'At dusk on Friday, 13 December 1907, the sailing ship *Thomas W Lawson* sank off the Scilly Isles in the English Channel.' This is the opening sentence of the book *The Attacker's Advantage*, by Richard N. Foster, a director at McKinsey. The *Thomas W Lawson*, a huge, cumbersome seven-masted schooner, was the symbol of a last vain attempt by the owners of sailing ships to assert themselves against the modern steamers that had taken much of the transport business from them. Instead of recognizing the signs of the times and moving with them, the owners of the *Thomas W Lawson* stubbornly chose to place their faith in the tried and tested methods of the past. But this last attempt to resist the forces of technological progress was inevitably doomed to failure. Foster says: 'The age of commercial sailing vessels ended with the *Thomas Lawson*, and from that moment on, the steamers ruled the seas.'

Some decades have passed since the *Thomas W Lawson* sank, yet sometimes you get the impression that its spirit still sails the waters of our business world. To put it in other words, there are still managers who cling tenaciously to outdated products, processes and attitudes instead of questioning the status quo critically and having the courage to think unconventionally and bring new, fresh ideas to their business activities.

Once they were champions, now they are forgotten

Take for example Zündapp, the Bavarian motorcycle manufacturer. The Zündapp models never held the fascination of a BMW or a Harley Davidson, but their mopeds were inexpensive and robust. Their advertisements promised 'Motorcycles for everyman'. In 1977, the company employed a workforce of 1,900 and produced 115,000 mopeds and motor-assisted bicycles. However, the management of the company failed to recognize the changes taking place around them until it was too late. Rapidly increasing insurance premiums and changes in legislation, making it compulsory for drivers of mopeds to take a driving test, sent sales plummeting. And competition from cheaper Japanese manufacturers made life no easier for Zündapp either. Like Horex, Adler, NSU, Maico and Kreidler before them, Zündapp was forced into liquidation in 1984.

The list of companies that remained blind to the changes taking place around them could be continued ad infinitum: the American computer manufacturer Digital Equipment is another example that comes to mind. This company was caught completely unaware by the development of the personal computer. In the year 1977, Ken Olson, the founder, president and managing director of Digital Equipment, made a statement which has become legendary: 'There is no reason for any individual to have a computer in his home.'

These examples illustrate that the 'Thomas Lawson Syndrome' is in fact an insidious disease which strikes companies blind and deaf. It enchains managers to the goose that laid the golden eggs yesterday, despite the fact that the poor animal is obviously on its last legs.

Beware the Thomas Lawson Syndrome

The Thomas Lawson Syndrome strikes whenever managers have become so accustomed to dealing with existing products and processes that they are complacent and literally blind to new ideas. Those who have successfully established themselves on an existing market are particularly susceptible. The danger is to become phlegmatic as the organization is gradually lulled into a false sense of security and hence the status quo is no longer questioned. It seems enough to merely keep improving one's products rather than keeping one's eyes, ears and mind open for new, radical and innovative ideas. And yet that is exactly what they should be doing – and at the same time, this is one of the most challenging tasks facing every industry.

The lesson is clear. Wherever managers are happy simply to maintain the status quo, believing themselves immune to the forces of change on the markets, we shall see the typical symptoms of the Thomas Lawson Syndrome appearing. The sales figures of today reflect decisions made yesterday. Markets do not react immediately; there is always a delay. Decisions that may bring success today will not necessarily do so tomorrow. Fighting tomorrow's battles with the successful products of today is no recipe for business success, no matter what the size or nature of the company. And so it is the task of top management to become business unconventionalists, to embody a readiness to embrace change and dynamism.

Surrounded by doubters?

In all fairness, it has to be admitted that this is not exactly easy. If it were, would you be reading this book? And the reason that it is so difficult is that the path to change is paved with the objections of the sceptics.

> The defenders of the status quo will doubtlessly tell you that it is not possible or necessary to implement your idea. After all, they are the people who established the status quo, and now they are under attack from you! And so, if you want to bring about a revolution, you must steadfastly ignore these arguments.
>
> Guy Kawasaki, marketing expert

And even when you have succeeded in overcoming the misgivings of the sceptics within your own company, the next challenge awaits you. Of course there are always risks if you deviate from what is the norm for your industry – and that is what business unconventionality is all about. But is there an alternative? We don't think so! If you want to establish something new, you are going to have to take risks.

Be prepared to sail against the wind

Within your own organization, too, you will encounter incomprehension and resistance. It is only natural that staff will become nervous when it seems that something they have been doing for years is being questioned. And it is only natural that sales staff will fear both the reactions of their existing customers and the extra work entailed in addressing new target groups. In many companies, strategy is geared to offering existing customers a better service rather than to finding completely new target groups. Another factor that makes innovation even more difficult is that the majority of management processes within companies are firmly in the hands of the defenders of the tried and tested. They cling to the products and strategies that have brought them success in the past, and are unwilling to take a risk and cast them aside. This places the burden of proving the potential of innovations firmly on you as a business unconventionalist, as you are the one challenging the status quo. This is an irony of fate when you consider that the risks involved in relying too firmly on maintaining an uncertain status quo are seldom, if ever, evaluated. As a business unconventionalist, the message that is conveyed to you in many different guises is that incremental improvements are infinitely preferable to genuine innovation – although in fact the opposite is more often the case.

As a business unconventionalist, you will have to overcome many obstacles. And it is obvious that your rivals are going to try to shoot you down when you dare to break with established rules. The best way to deal with all these sceptics is to question the overall strategy and to advocate a completely new philosophy. A comprehensive approach is far more difficult to find fault with than gradual changes, for example in a company's price, product or marketing models. So, let us immerse ourselves in the world of unconventional thinking and begin with a controversial topic.

The 360° view: glean inspiration from other industries

We see no problem with occasionally analysing what your competitors are up to. This is only sensible management practice. But it becomes a problem when managers have their eyes permanently and exclusively fixed on their rivals, like the rabbit staring, terror-stricken, at the snake. It is a problem because precious resources are squandered when managers, as if hypnotized, observe every step the competition takes and then slavishly copy them a short time later, thereby overlooking the fact that their rivals are themselves often bogged down in the past. And it is clear where this leads: it results in almost identical (which means interchangeable) products and services at almost identical prices.

Never underestimate the competition

But what happens when business unconventionalists break into such an environment with their fresh ideas? Interestingly enough, such sources of competition are often dismissed as insignificant, or looked down on. Just remember how the established television networks in the United States reacted to Ted Turner's announcement of his new idea for a 24-hour news channel: CNN was ridiculed as the 'Chicken Noodle Network' and Ted Turner was seen as a crackpot and not as a serious innovator.

The interesting question is, why didn't the established television stations pick up on this idea themselves? How come the established American stations ABC, NBC and CBS didn't introduce their own 24-hour news channels? Surely these giants could easily have shaken off an outsider like Turner? Presumably it would have been much easier for them to launch a new product in a new format, given their presence on the market, their financial clout and their technical know-how, than for a newcomer like Turner. But the opposite was the case.

Learning to forget is an important lesson for success

Many of the giants on the market barricade themselves behind a 'maintenance of the status quo' mindset, as we saw in the example of the Thomas Lawson Syndrome. The problem is that they become weighed down by the burden of their own past: the burden of a seemingly reassuring maintenance of the status quo at all costs, and an aversion to taking the risks inevitably involved in any form of innovation. And although the market conditions today are completely different from those of the past, and although the opportunities offered on future markets will differ considerably from those of the markets of today, these defenders of the status quo are all too quick to point out how successful their present products have been in the past, and will defend them tooth and nail when you suggest change.

> If you believe that a product will be a success, it is because you know and understand the concept already. But so do your competitors. Products that occupy new niches or form the basis for a whole new industry like FedEx, CNN, Post-it or Ziploc will usually be applied in fields which were unimaginable at the time of their launching. It's as simple as that.
>
> Tom Peters

Let us take a further example: the coffee shop chain Starbucks is a world-wide success story. In the United States, Starbucks is so successful that it has more loyal customers than any other retailer in the country. On average, a Starbucks customer visits a Starbucks 18 times per month. Where was Nestlé, the producer of Nescafé, the world's best-selling coffee, when Starbucks got going? Why didn't Nescafe come up with a concept for a world-wide network of trendy coffee bars? It knows the coffee market better than anyone else, after all. What were the people at Nestlé thinking about while the Starbucks chain was being established? Presumably they were debating the colour of their packaging or the shape of the jars to be placed on the supermarket shelves, or wondering how they could finally outpace their competitors at Procter & Gamble.

Why wasn't it existing companies that introduced these innovations? The answer is simple: they didn't even see the opportunity staring them in the face. And then, when outsider Howard Schultz launched Starbucks with a few coffee shops in Seattle, they didn't even realize that a new competitor was born.

Look again!

The truth is that the market leaders often think that the old-established companies are the enemy. However, they are looking in the wrong direction:

> Somewhere out there is a bullet with your company's name on it. Somewhere out there is a competitor, unborn and unknown, that will render your strategy obsolete. You can't dodge the bullet. You're going to have to shoot first.
>
> Gary Hamel, strategy guru and visiting professor at the London Business School

Figure 1.1 Starbucks: more than 8,500 coffeeshops worldwide and yet was overlooked by the competition.
Source: Starbucks Germany

Here lies the greatest danger – and at the same time your greatest opportunity. Take a look over the rim of the teacup of your own industry, take a full 360§ scan and pick out good and useful elements from different industries.

Rule 1 of business unconventionality

The 360° view: glean inspiration from other industries.

Conventional thinking: look for good and innovative ideas among your competitors and within your own industry.
Business unconventionality: deliberately look for ideas and inspiration for new products and services in totally different industries.

Companies are often geared primarily to competing with their rivals in their industry and beating them. The problem with this is that it makes the strategies, products and prices of companies competing in the same industry interchangeable. Subsequently, the only way for these companies to get an edge over their competitors is to compete with them on prices, processes or quality – or all three.

Place no limits on your thinking

The look over the rim of your teacup is what distinguishes companies that put innovative and unconventional thinking into practice from those with a conventional approach. Companies that think conventionally concentrate on their existing customers, and expend a lot of energy on finding new ideas to improve products or the overall marketing mix. This approach does indeed bring about improvement, but it will never produce pioneering innovations, nor will it make a company 'different' (in the positive sense) or help it to differentiate itself. In contrast, companies where business unconventionalists are at home will broaden their horizons: they create new markets, change the rules of the game and develop completely new products and business models. Such innovations can take the form of the establishment of new price categories or consist of as yet unheard-of quality of service, as we shall see in many of the examples to follow.

Thinking unconventionally requires a different strategic approach. Instead of thinking merely within the conventional limits of competition, managers must systematically look outside the box. This allows them to discover as yet unexploited terrain with potential for a true boost in value. To do so, managers need to forget the traditional limits of competition and focus their gaze on completely different industries, other strategic groups and consumer sectors, and complementary product and service ranges.

Transpose business models: the customs authorities learn from eBay

Let us now take a closer look at how business unconventionality can work in practice – even in a government department. With all due respect, we have to admit that we had always assumed a government department would be the last place you would find unconventional thinking. However, the example of the German customs authorities shows just how wrong that assumption was. German customs were looking for new ways to dispose of the many articles impounded or confiscated by them. In their search, they looked beyond the confines of their own sector to a completely different field: online auctions. More precisely, they found the inspiration for a new sales model in the activities of the online auction house eBay. Using the internet address www.zoll-auktion.de, almost 200 government agencies now auction off everything that is confiscated in the name of the state: cars, carpets, computers, electronic devices of all kinds, watches and clocks, angling equipment – even coffee and spirits.

What can this example teach us? Nowadays, companies – and this applies equally to government agencies – are increasingly forced to tread unconventional paths in order to reach their customers. Second, when you break with convention, whole new avenues open up: you have a temporary monopoly, you can establish your brand on a new market and set up a learning infrastructure which gives you the edge in the development of products and services for a new generation.

When we look at the history of companies such as CNN, Dell, Ikea and Swatch, we see that initially, they were all dismissed as oddballs by experts, analysts, rivals and customers, because they were breaking with tradition and reinventing the rules of the game. But these companies are also examples that illustrate that intuition, the readiness to innovate and a good portion of unconventional thinking are the basis of success. As Akio Morita, the founder of Sony, summed up his management philosophy, 'I do not serve markets. I create them.'

There is another factor that distinguishes these companies: the courage of their managers, who are prepared to tread new ground and are willing to take risks and to redefine the rules of their industry.

Customers are breaking with tradition – are you?

Perhaps you will be familiar with this attitude from your own family: The choice of the financial institution you banked with used to be taken as seriously as your choice of religion, and as in the case of your chosen faith, you just did not change banks like you changed your socks. From the point of view of the banks, the fact that customer loyalty to a particular financial institution was predominantly a matter of tradition was a heaven-sent gift. And so it is hardly surprising that in the past, banking has been characterized by tradition and adherence to strict rules. Some critics would maintain that this is still the case in some of our glass-fronted banking palaces today. On the customer side, however, there have been lasting changes.

Traditionally, customers did not change banks. Today the situation is different. Direct banking, which is increasingly opening up the market for foreign institutions, and of course online banking, have had a lasting effect on customer behaviour. In this field, lukewarm, over-cautious or copycat strategies will at best just about enable you to hold on to your position, and at worst be a recipe for failure.

If customers cannot clearly see what makes your product unique and innovative, you are heading for serious problems. Why? Because customers have higher and higher expectations. They want more, they want it faster, better and cheaper – and they want it on their conditions and according to their time schedules. Think about it: today, we expect much more of telephone companies and computer technology, and want much better service in hotels, than just five years ago. Is it surprising that marketing expert Regis McKenna claims our age is the age of the 'never satisfied customer'?

Process optimization: what the banks learnt from DaimlerChrysler

This means that banks – and not only banks – have to become even more professional in order to survive in the market. The provision of services in bank branches is an important sector, as it is extremely cost-intensive for the banks. Whether you look at Deutsche Bank, Bank of America, HSBC or Citibank, they are all looking for new ideas: and they have found them in the automobile industry. In order to remain competitive in future, banking processes have to be optimized, ration-alized and standardized. In addition, the companies need to concen-trate on their core competences. While banks usually create 80 to 90 per cent of their added value themselves, this figure is frequently below 30 per cent in the automobile industry.

Citibank showed the way. It hired consultants who had previously been involved in redesigning and optimizing processes at DaimlerChrysler. Their first conclusion: banking is a highly complex business. Second conclusion: the productivity of employees can be increased by 30 per cent with changes in personnel and a more effi-cient distribution of labour.

In Germany, Citibank has reduced its costs to an unparalleled level and now offshores many processes. For example, all international transactions are now processed in Dublin. This allows the Citibank group to cash in on its strengths by following the example of what has long been standard in the automobile industry.

A bank like a coffee shop: the Umpqua Bank in Oregon

Let us stay with the example of banking for a moment. Banks are not only learning from the automobile industry, but also from an industry which at first sight seems a very unlikely source of inspiration for financial institutions: coffee shop chains like Starbucks. Particularly in the United States, banks have adopted ideas from coffee shops on a large scale in their struggle against a problem which is also becoming increasingly acute in Europe: to re-establish ties of loyalty with customers. And so some financial institutions have done everything within their power to make banking with them a pleasurable experience: less high-tech, more personal touch. The Umpqua Bank in Oregon, for example, deliberately designed its branches in such a way that customers are tempted to stay there for longer than it takes to just withdraw some money or pay their bills – and it won the very prestigious IDEA Award, the Oscar for industrial design.

How can design turn a service into a pleasurable experience for customers? The revamped Umpqua branches look more like citizen's centres than financial institutions. Firstly, Umpqua realized that one of its customers' most important goals was to improve their quality of life, and that they were interested in seeing how far their bank could support them in this. And so Umpqua does all it can to invite its customers to spend more time in their bank, in an atmosphere more like that of a coffee bar than a traditional bank. Customers can drink coffee at their leisure. There are workstations with internet access. There is a postal service centre and a library with books, newspapers and magazines on financial topics. And of course, it offers extended opening hours on workdays, including Saturdays.

Umpqua has realized that customers will either perceive banking as a necessary evil, something to be done as quickly as possible online – or as a lifestyle decision. And Umpqua has tried, with considerable success, to make banking just such a lifestyle decision.

Figure 1.2 The Umpqua Bank – a lifestyle bank where customers love to linger
Source: Umpqua Bank, www.umpquabank.com

A bank as a life supporter: Washington Mutual

Washington Mutual, one of the most successful banks for private clients in the United States, has followed a similar course. In the space of 10 years, it has increased the number of its branches tenfold, from 250 to 2,500, and it aims to open a further 250 branches every year. Here, too, the focus is on a 'non-banking' strategy. Washington Mutual sees itself as an 'empathy-driven service bank for the man on the street'. Its employees are seen as 'life supporters' for their clients, advising customers on all services they might need – for example on college funds for their children. Each contact with customers takes the form of a personal chat. The result is an above-average cross-selling rate and a high degree of customer loyalty.

Also, Washington Mutual sees technology as a means not to minimize customer contact and further the self-service ideal, but to support its staff. You will also find books and software at Washington Mutual branches, and the bank offers seminars informing its customers on financial topics. The general emphasis is on establishing emotional ties – and the results prove the strategy right.

But establishing emotional ties with the customer is not the only factor that is going to play an increasingly important role in the future. Technology is also a crucial element: customers today are no longer at the mercy of production plans, product and promotion mixes and opening hours. Instead, they can choose from an endless variety of products and suppliers from all over the world. They can use the internet to gather any information they require, thereby strengthening their position of power immensely. The customers of tomorrow will be even better informed and even more proactive.

A new chance for old machines: GoIndustry

A company that relies on this important aspect of technology in conjunction with a clever unconventional-thinking approach is the Munich-based firm GoIndustry. Its basic idea: What do companies do with old machines they no longer require? What happens to the machinery when a company goes bankrupt? This is no small market: experts estimate the market for used capital investment goods at a volume of €44 billion per year. Traditionally, the machinery was sold off or auctioned locally. GoIndustry found a completely new scope for activity by looking further afield. Its model was eBay. It took the principle of internet auctions and applied it to the field of industrial auctions. Internet auctions offer significant advantages for the seller: an internet auction obviously attracts more interest than a local auction, so machines can often be sold for higher prices. And prospective buyers save time and money, as they no longer have to travel to buy machines.

In order to run such a business professionally, of course, you need the corresponding know-how. GoIndustry bought into the expertise of well-known auction houses by investing in traditional companies such as Henry Bucher (Great Britain), Michael Fox (United States) and Herbert Karner (Germany/Austria). And GoIndustry itself had the requisite online know-how.

GoIndustry is the brainchild of Herbert Willmy, a manager with decades of experience in the German 'old economy'. What made the company prosper was its successful blend of technology and classic auctioneering. It still needs its local staff, however: it employs 260 people in 16 countries, and with its widespread presence and solid customer database, it can directly target prospective clients in more than 30 countries.

Grow like McDonald's: lawyers on an expansion course

Taking courageous steps aimed at being the first on the market with unusual ideas and unique services generates the energy you need to carve out a niche for your company. This in turn produces the desired customer loyalty, the margins, the turnover and the market shares you require. If your aim is to be unique, you can also cash in on business models which have had a history of success in other industries and which will give you the edge in your own industry. What, for example, can lawyers learn from the business models of companies like McDonald's? They could of course diversify and offer their clients the usual legal services plus a double cheeseburger, but that is not what we mean here. Companies like McDonald's are examples of extremely successful franchising systems that function worldwide. For lawyers, the concept of franchising is of particular interest because it is becoming increasingly expensive to set up a legal practice from scratch, and because the legal services branch is subject to severe restrictions as

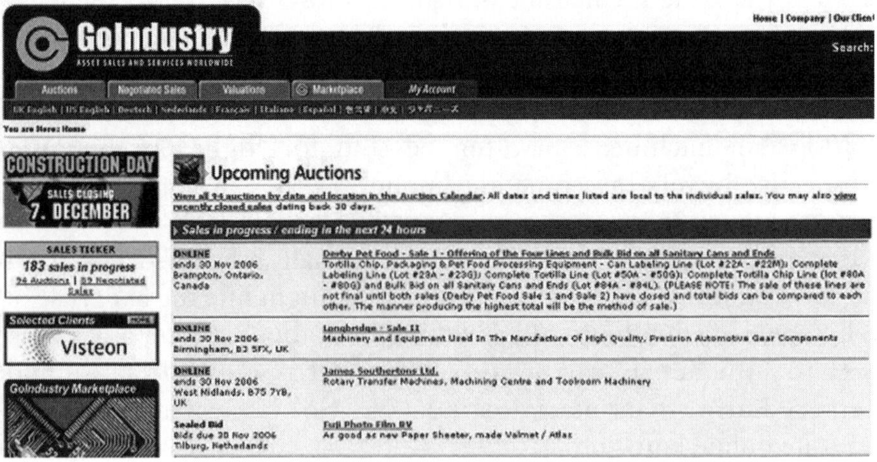

Figure 1.3 The GoIndustry website, marketing used machinery to a wider audience

Source: GoIndustry AG, www.goindustry.com

far as marketing is concerned. This is especially true outside the United States.

Legitas, a joint venture of independent legal practices from Hamburg, has picked up on an idea which has already proved very successful in other countries. Law firms, modelling themselves on the franchise system, join forces for marketing activities but retain their legal independence. Janolaw, from Sulzbach in Germany, goes one step further: it plans to open more than 120 'lawyer's stores' in German city centres over the next few years, and to offer the decisive advantage of ubiquitous presence and of low-price legal services. First consultations will cost only €49.90, a real bargain compared to the hourly fee of up to €180 that lawyers usually charge. The hourly fees will also be in the lower price range, at €75 – established law firms often charge several hundred euros. It remains to be seen whether the legal discounters will be a success story in Germany, but it is already clear that they are shaking the foundations of what is an extremely traditionally minded industry.

Take it easy – or what?

You don't become a market leader by making overly cautious decisions or giving polite answers. Neither will you reach the top by slavishly adhering to the advice of so-called experts or putting all your money on the newest hot trends that are usually no more than reflections of short-lived fads. Yet many managers are only too happy to pick up on the latest trends propagated in management literature, in the belief that this will provide them with an effective strategy that will transform them instantly into market leaders. They couldn't be more wrong!

If you want to reach the top, you need the courage to take risks and a daring and unconventional strategy. Stelios Haji-Ioannou is a businessman with just these properties – and he is successful because he swam against the stream. The son of a Greek shipowner, he borrowed £5 million from his father in 1995. Today, everyone in Great Britain knows him as Stelios, the head of the easyGroup. His story began with the foundation of the low-price airline easyJet. Low-price flights, ticket sales via the internet, service cut back to a minimum – this was his concept. In 1998 he founded the easyGroup, and in the meantime he has transferred this concept successfully to numerous other industries:

- At easyCar, British people can hire a car for as little as £3 per day.
- easyHotel offers accommodation in London starting at just £5 per night.
- At easyCinema, you can buy cinema tickets at discount prices via the internet.
- easyBus runs on overland routes within Great Britain. Prices start at £1 and tickets are bought over the internet.
- Looking towards the future, easyTelecom is poised to enter the telecommunications and mobile phone market with the same concept.

The big question for all the companies within the easyGroup is: how can we keep costs extremely low and at the same time dramatically boost capacity utilization and demand? The easyGroup has managed to do just that in all its operations. In addition to the cinemas, the airline, the car-rental company, the landline and mobile phone services and the bus company, the easyGroup also includes such widely varying operations as internet cafés, cruise liners, hotels, credit card companies and a pizza home delivery service – and there's no end to the expansion in sight!

Figure 1.4 What is the world coming to? easyCruise, the no-frills cruise line

Source: easyGroup, www.easycruise.com

Can hotels learn from low-price airlines?

The interesting thing about the easyGroup phenomenon is that Stelios Haji-Ioannou did not create any of these markets, but that his is the only company applying this business model so consistently on each market. As a business model, it is as old as it is simple: generally coveted goods are sold at a higher price and less desirable goods at a lower price. So it is not the idea in itself that is striking, but the fact that apparently no one thought of it before.

The Spanish NH Hotels Group borrowed an idea from the low-price airlines industry. It is presently in the process of changing its pricing system to one adapted from that of the cut-price flight operators. In its Munich hotels, the chain offers rooms according to the principle 'The earlier you book, the less you pay.'

The idea behind it is that rooms are available in different price brackets. They are reserved in the cheapest category first. Once there are no more rooms available in this price category, the price moves up to the next bracket, rising in six steps from €29 to €177 per night, excluding breakfast. The rooms in the cheapest category are prepaid by credit card. Bookings cannot be cancelled but can be changed for a fee of €10. The results after the initial test phase were that in the hotels where this system was tested, the average price paid per room and night did not decrease. On the contrary, the hotels received more bookings and profits rose.

These examples also illustrate that companies where innovators are at work will not hesitate to render their own structures and processes obsolete. They know that if they don't, someone else is going to do it for them.

Let us now look at another 'industry' which is currently struggling with its outdated image – or to put it another way, an industry where customers feel that the service offered is no longer in keeping with the requirements of modern-day life.

If the mountain won't come to Mohammed, the Mobile Confessional will come to you!

Banks and grocery stores showed the way: 'If the customer won't come to us, then we have to go to the customer.' How? By putting the bank or the store on four wheels and driving to the consumer.

Churches in Western Europe are faced with dwindling congregations, not to mention the falling numbers of those going to confession. In order to remedy this situation, the German Catholic organization 'Kirche in Not' decided to take an unusual step. Under the motto 'Confession made easy', it set up the Mobile Confessional, a specially equipped VW camper van in which priests take confession 'on tour'.

The Mobile Confessional service was established under the auspices of the Bishop of Eichstätt, Dr. Walter Mixa, and it is available to parishes and religious communities free of charge. The aim of the project is to give people the opportunity to speak to a priest, to obtain spiritual counsel or, if desired, to confess and obtain absolution, not only at organized events such as the World Youth Conference but also in the course of their everyday lives, in public places.

Business unconventionality box

It is more profitable to leave the well-trodden paths than simply to imitate other companies.

The examples in this chapter show that we all have a tendency to look in the old familiar places for solutions to problems. That is only normal. We all move more confidently in terrain we know, and we believe that we only have to dig deep enough in order to find the answers we need. Yet we should not be surprised if, even after extensive and painstaking excavations, we are left still waiting for that decisive breakthrough.

The solution: take a look elsewhere and combine the new with the familiar! Search completely foreign fields for ideas, inspiration and suggestions for new products and services.

Remember the German customs authorities, who learnt from the example of the online auction house eBay, and the Umpqua Bank, which drew great inspiration from the coffee shop idea. Instead of being a bank in the conventional sense, it aims to be a 'third place' for its customers, a place somewhere between their place of work and their own living room.

Or think of the Catholic Church – it too found new ideas in other fields: in banks and mobile grocery stores. The result: the Mobile Confessional is 'on tour'.

Dead centre: get out of those middle-of-the-market segments – fast!

Many companies have settled themselves down comfortably in the middle of the market. If you ask about their target groups, they will say that they aim to cater to the needs of 'the whole market', according to the motto 'Something for everyone'. But in those mid-market segments, in the grey zone of mediocrity, the space is getting cramped. There's no room to breathe, or, to put it another way, you won't grab the customers' attention. They won't even notice you, because there's more and more competition in the middle of the market, as profit margins are dwindling and there is hardly any difference in the quality of the goods and services on offer, which all broadcast the same message to the consumer.

The middle of the market is dying, slowly disappearing. It is no longer enough to offer a little bit of everything to everyone, as customers are increasingly becoming more and more individualized and demanding. And so the second rule of business unconventionality is truly a question of survival.

Rule 2 of business unconventionality

Dead centre: get out of those middle-of-the-market segments – fast!

Conventional thinking: the target group for your products or services should be as wide as possible. Your range needs to be not too expensive, not too cheap and of interest to as many people as possible.
Business unconventionality: get out of the dead centre of the market. Define yourself and your products, and assume a clear position outside the middle of the market (premium range or discount), where there is still money to be made.

The consumer goods market is a prime example of increasing polarization. The discount and luxury goods sectors are seeing above-average growth rates, while the middle of the market is losing ground fast. This is a trend that is particularly evident in many consumer goods sectors. And the winners are not always those who focus on 'cheaper is better'.

The art of letting go

Yet although many companies are perfectly aware of this development, they fail to react to it. Why? Well, how likely is it that a company will abandon an existing area of activity – even if the success rate is below average – unless it can see a few promising alternatives? Just take a look at your own company. When was the last time you opted to stick with the tried and tested procedure or the familiar situation, even though you knew that there might be a much better alternative?

The answer is quite simple. You need to have a few really convincing options up your sleeve before you will be prepared to let go of the established routines and procedures you are clinging to. But it is not always easy to find these alternatives. Just imagine, for example, that you run a bakery. Of course you will have noticed that your customers have become increasingly price-conscious. On the other hand, you also see that they don't think twice about paying €6 for a glass of latte macchiato and an Italian pastry. So what do you do? You try to satisfy both needs. You save on staff or buy even cheaper ingredients. At the same time, you set up a little 'Coffee Corner' where you sell latte macchiato and other coffee specialities. In other words, you waste a lot of effort trying to perform a difficult balancing act between the cheap and the exclusive.

Business unconventionalists, however, have a different way of looking at things: they learn to see things from a different perspective, to be different and take up a clear stance.

The air is getting increasingly rare in the middle of the market. Act now!

Business unconventionality is about more than just a change of perspective – it has a lot to do with courage. It's the courage to take up a clear stance instead of trying to offer 'Something for everyone': to be *either* a self-service bakery with fresh bread at discount prices *or* a premium bakery offering top-of-the-range goods at correspondingly higher prices. Because one thing is clear: the average bakery offering average products to anyone out there will at most be able to keep its head above water – and only with tremendous effort.

The necessity to take up a clear stance can be seen in many industries. It is more and more difficult for middle-of-the-road companies to create excitement with customers. Just take a look around you:

hairdressing chains offering inexpensive haircuts are increasingly popular, while the more upmarket hairstylists have also carved out a niche ('Because you're worth it'). In the middle of the market, however, the air is becoming increasingly rare. Take discount airlines as an example. They have conquered an amazing share of the market. People who used to travel through Europe by bus now simply hop on a plane. And it's not only the notorious penny-pinchers who do so! On the contrary: You only paid €49 for your flight to Milan, so you can afford to go on a shopping spree and invest the money you saved in a handbag from Prada.

No matter how the economy is doing: there's always a market for luxury

Let's stay with the example of the airlines for a moment. At the opposite end of the spectrum from the increasing number of low-price airlines there is another interesting development. Companies offering luxury services such as private aircraft for managers are enjoying increasing popularity, despite the continuing atmosphere of economic gloom. The Teal Group, a team of US consultants, even sees the upswing in the private air travel sector as the beginning of a lasting boom – far above the current upswing in the global economy. Experts predict the sale of about 6,500 business jets worth approximately US$92 billion over the next decade. And what's going on in the middle of the market? Airlines such as Alitalia and others are fighting for survival.

Coffee machines for the lifestyle-conscious

Are you still using your trusted filter coffee machine for your breakfast coffee? Sorry, but if you do, you are hopelessly out of date. Espresso machines are a must-have nowadays: that is, machines that cost the equivalent of a week's holiday in Italy. Sales in this sector have increased more than five-fold since 1996. Some manufacturers were quick to recognize the trend – or did they in fact create it?

High-end luxury machines such as the Impressa S9 Avantgarde, which costs around €1,400, are among the best-selling models made by Swiss premium manufacturer Jura. You can get a simple coffee machine for €15 from your local discount store, so for the price of one Impressa S9 you could buy almost 100 coffee machines. Or enough coffee to last you several years. Or you could drink 450 latte macchiatos in the trendiest coffee bar in town ...

But – and this is the intriguing fact – the Impressa S9 is in a completely different market. It would not stoop to the level of a common filter coffee machine. Instead, it engenders the quintessence of espresso culture, promises heavenly aroma and an unforgetable coffee experience – and gives you the aura of an authentic barista when entertaining friends and acquaintances. Real enjoyment is more than just a cup of coffee! So Jura and other manufacturers of high-end

Figure 1.5   The Impressa S9 Avantgarde – a coffee machine becomes a status symbol

Source: Jura AG, www.juraworld.com

coffee machines are in fact selling not just a machine that makes coffee, but primarily image and lifestyle. In addition, there is also an interesting market for the side-products of espresso culture: cups, glasses, whisks, for example, to name but a few of the products no kitchen can do without. A whole industry profits from this lifestyle trend in the premium segment.

The Swiss premium manufacturer Jura is just one example from a whole range of outstanding companies operating very successfully in the market. The list could be continued ad infinitum, but the message would be the same: if Jura had simply concentrated on providing its customers with a warm, caffeinated beverage, it would presumably still be happily selling inexpensive filter coffee machines. What makes Jura an outstanding company, however, is that it created a market for something its customers didn't even realize they needed. Or could you have imagined 10 years ago that you would seriously consider spending €1,400 on a machine that makes coffee? Jura does more than simply satisfy the need for a good cup of coffee, and it is precisely that which creates growth rates that other firms can only dream of.

Potential in the grey zone

The key to business unconventionality and the resulting competitive edge does not lie solely in the creation of demand, but also in being the first on the market with a new, unusual, pioneering product, service or business plan. Markets with a large grey zone in the middle are ideal. The bakery sector is a good example. The pioneer of self-service bakeries, Robert Kirmaier from the German town of Monheim,

Table 1.1 Predicted development of market shares

Market shares 1980	
Low-price products:	24%
Mid-price segment:	49%
Top of the range products:	27%
Market shares 2010	
Low-price products:	40–45%
Mid-price segment:	10–20%
Top of the range products:	40–45%

Source: Study by BAT Freizeit-Forchungs-Institut, 2001

founder of the BackWerk company, opened the first self-service bakery in Germany. The tremendous success of the discount bakeries shows that his instinct was sound. One could even say that he accelerated the polarization of the market, as BackWerk and many copycat companies now cater to the more price-conscious customer. Their prices are unbeatable. There is no service, no specialist staff, no advice provided, but they offer fresh-baked bread, rolls and cookies all day long. Discount bakeries are successful thanks to the price, the freshness of the produce and the time-saving through self-service.

This does not mean, however, that all consumers like the idea. There are people who are willing to pay up to €1.50 for a 24-grain super-healthy bread roll. Organic and health products are not for the penny pinchers and there is a substantial segment out there in the market that is willing to pay premium prices for premium products.

Alternatively, take a look at the automobile sector. DaimlerChrysler introduced the Maybach, a luxury Rolls-Royce class limousine – and found a market for it with the help of clever sales methods tailored to the target group. As each car is unique and is produced to the specifications of the buyer, there is a specially trained team of 'personal liaison

Figure 1.6 Backwerk – the self-service bakery
Source: BackWerk Systemzentrale GmbH & Co KG

managers' to help the celebrity clientele decide on the details of their unique Maybach limousine. From the choice of wooden veneer on the humidor to the position of the television screen or a dashboard decorated with brilliant-cut diamonds, almost any wish can be accommodated. Premium models from other car makers were not nearly as successful, one of the reasons being that the target group for such luxury limousines is relatively small and that DaimlerChrysler does whatever it takes to please this very demanding clientele.

DaimlerChrysler, like BMW, has been successful in expanding its product portfolio by introducing lower-priced models for first-time buyers, making a Mercedes or a BMW affordable for new target groups. This is market expansion and image transfer 'downwards'. And so the campaign for the BMW 1 Series, with which the Munich company addressed the target group for smaller cars such as the VW Golf, became the greatest product campaign in the history of BMW.

Premium products for the masses: Häagen-Dazs

However, the success story of the coffee-shop chain Starbucks and the premium-range ice cream manufacturer Häagen-Dazs is based on a different strategy. These companies target the broad mass of consumers, but with a premium-range product – in one case coffee, in the other ice cream. These companies developed a completely new product for a mass market and thereby created a new market and a temporary monopoly which in turn helped them to realize above-average profits.

Both companies consciously decided against supplying the medium and low-price segments of the market and went straight for the high-end prices. By following this strategy, they dramatically raised the bar, in product presentation, customer experience and so on, for a whole industry. It does not matter whether you are in the high-price, middle- or low-price segment. Customers have come to expect this standard. This becomes evident when you look at the design of the countless me-too coffee-shop concepts and the packaging and naming of ice cream.

The situation becomes problematical when companies cannot make up their minds. There are cases where companies have successfully managed to sell both a low-price and a premium range, but the differentiation between the two product ranges must be transparent to the consumer – and the two ranges must be clearly separate. It is common, in particular in the food sector, for manufacturers of branded goods to also sell to the discount stores, but in different packaging and under the strictest secrecy. If such collaboration becomes known, the premium manufacturers might suffer losses because of the difference in price, or the fact that the difference in quality between their premium range and the products supplied to the discount chains is not perceptible. Discretion is therefore of the utmost importance if they do not want the buyers of their premium-range products to feel cheated.

Image boost for H&M: consumers fight to get a genuine Lagerfeld

Haute couture meets the hoarders: in autumn 2004, hundreds stormed H&M (Hennes & Mauritz) stores to get their hands on genuine designer fashion from Karl Lagerfeld. There was pushing and shoving reminiscent of the closing of the summer sales, as consumers grabbed for the articles, often without even looking at them. What was going on? Once again, 'Karl the Great', as Lagerfeld is known, was causing a stir. In 500 of Swedish retailer H&M's 1,000 stores worldwide, about 30 articles from Lagerfeld's exclusive designer collection – 20 for women and 10 for men – were on sale. The Swedish textile chain stressed repeatedly that the 'Lagerfeld for H&M' selection was strictly a limited edition, while cleverly omitting to name the exact number of each garment available. The result was hype, hysteria and shopping frenzy. After just two days, there were only a few articles from the collection still to be found in the stores. Instead, customers could now buy them on eBay – at a much higher price.

By cooperating with the textile chain, which is well known for its copies of designer fashion items, the star designer revolutionized the fashion industry – at least a little. In an interview with the German newspaper *Welt am Sonntag*, Lagerfeld emphasized that this was a logical step for him:

> One should not despise the 'masses'. One has a duty to make suggestions that can help to introduce a new idea of style …. Today, there are only two classifications: affordable and not affordable. And both have to be fashionable …. I play with the contrast between the two. I create haute couture for Chanel, an activity that is not affected by my work for H&M. This forces me to make an even greater effort in the high-end sector and to make my quality standards even higher. I see both fields as a challenge.

Lagerfeld is aware of the fact that the aim of the cooperation is an image transfer for H&M. The Swedish chain is keen to profit from the attraction of the name Lagerfeld, and its aim is always to be a little different and a little better than its competitors.

Gaining a competitive edge through uniqueness: the winner takes all!

This is exactly what you need to do: do something new, something that is different from what your competitors are already doing. You need innovation that, at least for a short time, will give you the competitive edge that comes from offering something unique.

Regrettably, in many companies there is the tacit conviction that it is better to be quick off the mark in copying someone else than to aim for the competitive edge that unique status will give you. This arises from the assumption that being a pioneer is a very risky business. But is that really the case? Is it really safer to quickly copy others than to be the first one to offer something new and completely different? Of course, being the 'first mover' does involve a certain financial risk – but it is a question of making creative use of scanty resources and minimizing the risks involved. And that is the challenge and the path to being innovative while still keeping the potential financial risk as low as possible.

What exactly do you need to do to gain that competitive edge? Some years ago, it would have sufficed to add a few extras to an existing product. That is not enough today. Why? Because your competitors will have copied those extras within just a few days. Just take the automobile industry as an example. There is no such thing as a bad car any more, they are all good! No matter which car maker you look at, whether it's Toyota, Renault, Volkswagen or any of the others, nowadays they all have state-of-the-art technology. They all have large R&D departments whose job it is to improve on existing technology and to develop new technologies, new materials and even more fuel-efficient cars. And another thing: they all know their competitors' products inside out. They take their rivals' models apart and examine every detail. This means that in the automobile industry, the areas where it is possible for one company to stand out from the rest must lie elsewhere. In today's markets, it is no longer a question of who has the more powerful engine or the lower air drag coefficient. The area of differentiation lies elsewhere: design, service, image and people are important factors. And it is a question of distancing yourself from the grey zone of mediocrity and doing something that will take your rivals by surprise.

From nobody to the perfect body: Bruno Banani

Do the unexpected – that is the credo of the Bruno Banani Underwear GmbH, from Chemnitz in Saxony. 'We're always doing something no one expected,' says Wolfgang Jassner, the company's founder. 'Not for everybody' is the company's marketing slogan. And this is what they do: Each month a new model of Bruno Banani underwear goes on sale. Each model is produced in a limited edition, thus keeping the articles in artificially short supply and making Bruno Banani underpants a desirable collector's item for Banani fans.

Before Bruno Banani appeared on the scene, men's underwear was not particularly 'exciting'. But this company triggered a real cult, partly thanks to its unconventional promotion methods. For example, Bruno Banani underwear has successfully proved its tensile strength and good fit in space, in nuclear research centres and under deep-sea conditions.

Figure 1.7 Bruno Banani – underwear as a lifestyle product
Source: Bruno Banani

The Bruno Banani success story shows something else: the way out of the mid-market segments, away from the grey zone of mediocre products, does not necessarily mean that you have to conquer the luxury or discount segments. Bruno Banani chose a different strategy: the company has positioned itself outside the grey zone by consciously striving to be different, and has conquered a niche in the German market. Men have always had the choice between functional underwear and expensive garments from designers like Calvin Klein. But for a long time, there was nothing in between the functional fine-rib and the designer underwear, until a textile company from Saxony came along and filled the niche. The idea behind Bruno Banani? Designer underwear at affordable prices, to create a desirable home-produced fashion item as an alternative to the boring array of cheap underpants from the Far East. And what rounded the concept off perfectly was the name Bruno Banani, the brainchild of marketing agency Plenum Stoll & Fischbach.

An important point for the company is to ensure that Bruno Banani never becomes a mass-produced article. With this strategy, it now has an annual turnover of around €40 million. And while it started out producing only men's underwear, it has now successfully applied the concept to the women's underwear market, too.

Find new distribution concepts: a taste of the sweet life with Häagen-Dazs

The 'democratization of luxury' is another interesting way of breaking out of the grey zone. Since introducing its products to the German market in 1987, the Häagen-Dazs company has skilfully established its ice cream as a premium product, not only thanks to its high quality, but also by applying a well thought-out distribution concept. Haagen-Dazs ice cream is available in selected supermarkets, but above all, the company targeted home delivery services and petrol stations to ensure direct access to consumers. As a result of the limited selection available in such outlets, there is far less competition.

In addition to these distribution channels, there are also Häagen-Dazs cafés in Germany, Austria and Switzerland, run under a franchise system. This reinforces the image of Häagen-Dazs as a premium ice cream. The company plans to more than triple the number of cafés over the next few years. Their concept is successful: contrary to the general trend in the sector, Häagen-Dazs has seen double-digit growth rates for years.

Challenge established concepts!

The companies we describe in this chapter, have skilfully manoeuvred themselves out of the dead centre of the market. They have broken with established conventions. Business unconventionalists challenge established concepts and change them instead of striving to maintain the status quo.

There is a further interesting insight to be gained here: every strategy is valid only for a certain length of time. The key to success for executives and organizations alike, lies in promoting flexibility, adaptability, a constant learning process, the willingness to take risks, creative thinking and personal responsibility in order to profit from the forces in action around us, instead of taking the easy path of clinging to the familiar. The next two examples are an impressive demonstration of the fact that this strategy is also feasible for old-established companies – and that even the most unsophisticated product can become a cult object.

Birkenstock: from tree-hugger footwear to a fashion must-have

In the 1970s and 1980s, Birkenstock sandals for men and women were exactly the same, the anti-fashion footwear for members of the back-to-nature movement. In everyone's minds, they were firmly established as the standard footwear of anti-nuclear campaigners, peace protesters and supporters of Waldorf educational theory. No matter how comfortable they were, you didn't want to be seen wearing them to take the rubbish out. Without a trace of elegance, they made even the slenderest of feet seem unnaturally wide. From size 7 upwards you could easily use them to stamp out a camp fire.

But Birkenstock managed to turn that image around – and suddenly, healthy footwear from Birkenstock became a cult fashion accessory all over the globe. What happened? The company realized that the key for success lay in combining the aspects of health and design. In the early 1990s, two designers (Marc Jacobs and Randolph Duke) made this clumpy classic sandal into an elegant shoe for evening wear (with glitzy rhinestone buckles) and thus acceptable in fine society. The new image was further promoted by engaging supermodel Heidi Klum and actor Til Schweiger to appear in advertising campaigns.

Figure 1.8 Birkenstock – Heidi Klum proves that deep-footbed sandals can be sexy

Source: Birkenstock Orthopädie GmbH, www.birkenstock.com

And the new positioning worked: In America, celebrities started to wear these ultra-comfy sandals from Germany, even at evening and society events. After all, the heel cup and the patented footbed made of cork, jute and natural rubber ensure good blood circulation in the feet and do not constrict the toes. And that can be of priceless value when you're standing around at endless cocktail parties! In London there are waiting lists for the 'deep footbed sandal' and people queue in front of the store in the trendy shopping quarter Covent Garden. Even fashion maniac Victoria Beckham is said to have waited patiently for an hour to purchase a pair with light blue straps and white buckles. And that is not a PR gimmick – it really happens!

Jägermeister: the stag's head logo storms the trendy bar scene

The familiar bottle with the picture of the stag on the label was already around in the 1930s. Jägermeister was traditionally a popular digestif for the over-50s. But that was not enough for the strategists of the company from Wolfsbüttel in Lower Saxony.

In 1973, it persuaded German Football League team Eintracht Braunschweig to replace the traditional lion on its football shirts with the stag's head logo and to wear Jägermeister orange as the team colour. Thus Jägermeister was a pioneer of football team sponsorship, a practice that is commonplace nowadays – but in 1973 it had to fight the German football association in court to do so.

Today, Jägermeister still very skilfully manages to keep people talking about its herbal liqueur and is equally successful in introducing new, young target groups to the taste. Jägermeister is drunk in trendy bars, as a long drink with freshly pressed orange juice or on the rocks. Around 1,000 'Jägerettes' visit bars and clubs on promotional tours, not only in Germany, but also in the United States. The stag's head logo transcends all borders.

The company's advertising also mirrors how it is constantly refreshing and modernizing its image. The two stags from its commercials, Rudi and Ralph, were given a facelift. They were transformed from cuddly soft toys to amusing computer animations. The Jägermeister website is trendy and flashy, and in the online shop you can purchase sauna towels and g-strings in saucy designs.

The family-run business knows that the only way to achieve growth is to leave the dead centre of the market. It focuses its attention on one single brand and its marketing. Jägermeister ploughs about 19 per cent of its net turnover into advertising and marketing, concentrating on maintaining good connections with trade and gastronomy. It spends 70 per cent of the budget on the Jägerettes, whose next 'gigs' are announced on the internet. And above all, Jägermeister works against conventions – with a constant flow of new ideas, new activities in collaboration with other companies and celebrities. Jägermeister knows that the moment you rest on your laurels, you have already lost. That's why the company is careful to ensure that Jägermeister schnapps never becomes a mainstream drink. And Jägermeister is flexible: In Castro, an area of San Francisco where many gay men live, there is a team of 'Jäger Dudes' on tour instead of the Jägerettes. Jägermeister is always ready to move with the times!

Turn your radar on and reconsider who your competitors are

It doesn't matter whether you make schnapps, screws or underwear: Confining yourself to simply keeping an eye on your competition and analysing their activities renders you blind to radically new business ideas, and makes you overlook companies that have not traditionally been regarded as your rivals. They will be only too happy to take advantage of your temporary blindness. The music industry is a good example, although it is a negative one. Believing that their traditional business model was invincible, the music industry focused on analysing the strengths, weaknesses and management decisions of other recording companies.

But the dramatic downturn in sales tells a different story. Nowadays it is even difficult for the music industry to identify its rivals. Are mobile phones, computer games or other entertainment products competition? This would indicate that the recording companies' target group has remained essentially the same, primarily children and young people. And so, logically, its greatest rival remains the internet with its music file exchanges. In the United States, around 600 users of internet music exchanges have been prosecuted, and there are plans to follow suit in Germany. But will a flood of prosecutions really solve the problems of the music industry? We don't think so! The fact remains that the decision makers in the music industry – and not only there – need to come up quickly with new ideas for innovative business models, and find out how to reinvent their market.

Business unconventionality box

Quote: While everything is getting better, it is also becoming more and more uniform.

Paul Goldberger, architecture critic for the *New York Times*

Get out of the dead centre! Take a clear stance, position yourself carefully and take advantage of the polarization of the market segments (premium segment, discount segment), because that's where the profit is. Take a critical look at your range of products and services. Whereabouts in the market are you? Are you reaping the benefits of discount positioning, or are you focusing on the medium price and quality segments? Analysing the positioning of your company is vital to allow you to see clearly where and for what you stand.

It is not a copy of a product or service, but a variation or a completely new or improved product or service that will give you a clear profile.

Think of discount bakeries like BackWerk, which cleverly differentiated themselves from the anonymous mass of conventional bakeries with unbeatably low prices. Or think of underwear manufacturer Bruno Banani, which skilfully positioned itself between fine-rib underwear on one side and expensive designer underwear on the other, with an intriguing strategy: designer underwear at affordable prices with a built-in coolness factor. 'Not for everybody' is their advertising slogan, and it also aptly describes the strategic alignment of the company.

Travel light: cut the ballast

Companies that apply the rules of business unconventionality consistently are not likely to succumb to the temptation of trying to have their cake and eat it. They have a clear focus, and concentrate on one area, or just a few core areas, in which they are world-class. That is just about the opposite of what we normally mean by the term 'large business group' – where the word large refers not only to the turnover, but also to its diversified business activities. These enterprises dabble in many different industries and hope for the knock-on effects that are supposed to come about through the combination of diversified operations. But their strategy doesn't always work out. Remember, for example, former head of Daimler-Benz Edzard Reuter, who was bent on pursuing his illusory dream of an integrated technology group, a dream that was abruptly abandoned as soon as he was replaced by his successor Jürgen Schrempp. Or think of Nokia, one of the market leaders in the mobile telephone sector. Its rapid rise to fame was only possible because the company rid itself of its excess baggage: until 20 years ago, Nokia also produced paper, wellington boots, tractor tyres and garden hoses.

Business unconventionalists choose a different path: big is not always beautiful. Instead, you concentrate on those sectors in which you have the edge on the rest of the global market.

Rule 3 of business unconventionality

Travel light: Cut the ballast.

Conventional thinking: try to carry out as many profit-making activities as possible under your own steam.
Business unconventionality: focus on the activities where you are really world-class and leave the rest to suppliers, partners – or your own customers!

But concentrating on just a few business areas is not enough. Every process, no matter how insignificant, and every activity of your company must be subjected to careful examination. You must ask yourself: are we really world-class here? If not, it would be better to outsource it – to others who can do it better. Take Microsoft. Its games console X-Box is built entirely outside the Microsoft Corporation, leaving Microsoft free to focus on its strengths without having to acquire additional extensive hardware know-how. The most important thing is to ensure that you outsource the right functions – and find a competent partner.

The big names show you how it's done

In the automobile industry, only 35 per cent of a new car on average is produced by the car makers themselves. The rest is manufactured by suppliers. And this figure is likely to fall as far as 23 per cent over the next 10 years. The parts manufactured by suppliers are above all the car body, sheet metal parts, paintwork, chassis and modules, but outsourcing of the manufacture of other parts is also increasing.

Or take Puma. This sports equipment manufacturer and lifestyle company concentrates on its core competencies, which are innovation, design and marketing. The business is run from modest headquarters in Herzogenaurach with few hierarchy levels. Production and almost the entire logistics operations are carried out by partner companies. Distribution has been delegated to subsidiaries of the company. Customers, producers, distributors and franchisees are 'linked' via information and communications technology, thus creating a network of independent units which are perceived from the outside as one entity producing its own branded goods.

And by the way, Adidas, Nike, Reebok and Benetton have a similar structure. Coincidence? Probably not! They have all cut their ballast in order to 'travel light', as we called it at the beginning of this section. In a sector where competition is keen, they remain light-footed and extremely flexible. All excess baggage has been cast overboard, leaving these companies free to concentrate on what they are really good at.

Companies on the road to success: recognizing core competencies

The term 'core competency' does not refer to a particular individual skill or technology, but to a collection of skills and technologies that contribute to a large degree to the value of your company as perceived by your customers.

What is your company really good at? Where are you better than the competition and have gained such a competitive edge that no one is likely to catch up with you any time soon? Finding answers to these questions is a very valuable exercise, mainly for two reasons. First, it may not be clear to you what the core competencies of your company are. And second, you may realize that your strengths are not where you (and perhaps your customers, staff and suppliers) thought they were, but lie in a completely different area.

Take the global leader in network solutions for the internet, Cisco Systems, as an example. It's a high-tech company whose core competency you would expect to lie in a mastery of specific Internet technologies – but you would be wrong!

> Nowadays, 50 per cent of our products no longer come into contact with a Cisco factory or Cisco employees. They are assembled and distributed as if by magic by our suppliers, and the customers never even realize that we haven't touched them.
>
> Howard Charney, Senior Vice-President, Cisco

Cisco does not see its core competence in the technology sector:

> We've let go of the belief that our core asset is having two photons that do this or that. Our core assets are our ability to move fast, satisfy customer needs, be first to market and leverage our distribution channel. Once those assets are in place, then much of the technology development can effectively be outsourced just like we might outsource some basic manufacturing.
>
> (quoted in Hamel, 2000)

Lean to the extreme

What is the core competency of a bicycle manufacturer? British cycle producer Strida has found its own answer to this question: Strida's core competency lies in all strategic aspects of the business, in other words in looking after key accounts, marketing, product development and resource management. No more – and no less. And to do that, you only need a team of two: the owner and a banker to take care of financing.

The company owner, Steedman Bass, bought the design for a folding bicycle from a student. The bike consists of very few parts, and it can be erected and folded back up in just 15 seconds. The bikes are manufactured by the Ming Cycle Company in Taiwan, which purchases the parts from suppliers in China and does the assembly. Another outsourcing partner in Birmingham is responsible for marketing, logistics support, distribution to dealers and accounting.

Steedman Bass takes care of the strategic side of the business: key accounts, marketing, product development and resource management. So at Strida, the virtual enterprise has become a reality. The organization consists of many individual units, each fully independent, and all linked together to form a network. Above all, without this virtual structure, there would be no Strida bicycle. And because each part of the network is free to concentrate on its area of core competency, the network, as the sum of all its parts, is successful.

The folding bicycle is a success. It is popular with city dwellers who don't want to take the car, and also with the owners of yachts and motor homes, who find it practical to take another, smaller means of transport with them. And Strida makes a turnover of over €1 million.

Figure 1.9 Strida's folding bicycle – not suitable for the Tour de France, but extremely practical

Source: Strida UK Ltd, www.strida.com

Low-ballast management development

The structure of the glass manufacturing company Schott in Mainz, Germany is not quite as lean, but still very effective. The company realized that management development and training is not one of its core competencies, and thus hired the training and consulting firm Kommunikations-Kolleg AG Beratung & Training, which has a permanent staff of 22 and 200 freelancers that takes care of personnel development for clients all over the world.

And so Kommunikations-Kolleg AG carries out various training and personnel development programmes for Schott and other clients. Schott simply selects the members of its staff who are to participate in the programmes – and foots the bill. And because Kommunikations-Kolleg AG is focusing on its core competence, doing what it is best at, the system is more effective than many personnel departments. It defines the training requirements, hires the trainers, carries out quality control, books conference facilities and conducts the training programmes. As a result, the human resources management teams at companies like Schott are relieved of some of their many responsibilities, freeing personnel managers to concentrate on strategy and conceptualization, the management of suppliers and the implementation of effective control systems.

Let the customers do some of the work for you!

There are many different ways for a company to cast off excess baggage. Work processes can be delegated to suppliers, but that is only the beginning. Firms such as Strida or Puma, which have retained only their strategic core competences within the company itself, show that it is possible to do much more than simply delegate tasks to suppliers. And there is another interesting way to achieve a leaner structure: Ikea shows us how. Ikea customers buy their furniture and then transport, assemble and set it up themselves. In return, the customers save money! Banks have also applied this principle, outsourcing some services directly to their customers through the introduction of self-service internet banking and cash dispensers.

Business unconventionality box

Focus on the areas where you are really world-class and let your suppliers, partners or your own customers do the rest!

Business unconventionalists will not insist on retaining control over the entire value creation chain and doing as much as possible themselves. They realize the advantages of outsourcing processes that are not core competencies. Business unconventionalists may not create a complete value creation chain, but they will always occupy a central position in one.

Think of sports equipment manufacturer Puma. Puma focuses on its core competencies, namely development, design and marketing, and leaves everything else to its partners. British bicycle manufacturer Strida has taken this principle even further. Strida has only two employees, the owner of the company and a banker who takes care of the financing. Everything else is taken care of by partners in Taiwan and Birmingham.

2 Different thinking: markets

The strongest and most lasting solutions are those that continually lead to new products and new markets. Business unconventionalists such as CNN, Ikea, Body Shop, FedEx, Zara or Dell Computer didn't simply adapt to suit the market. On the contrary, they lead the market. In fact they created it, with revolutionary new products, services and business models. They are not steered by the market, they steer the market. They don't simply sit still and wait for the customers to come to them, they lead their customers into the future!

Accept no imitations – accept no limitations!

How did these business unconventionalists get where they are today? First and foremost, they were daring. They realized that in today's markets, it's a greater risk to be conventional than unconventional. And they have other things in common, too: these companies did not rely primarily on traditional management tools such as strategic planning, market research, competition analysis, customer surveys to get where they wanted to be. This is in marked contrast to the way conventional companies work. They will commission umpteen market research studies, observe the market carefully and watch closely to see which way their rivals are moving, before they take the risk of doing something new. They want to be absolutely sure that they have thought of every eventuality and weighed up every potential risk. Then – and only then – will they be prepared to take the next step.

They are coming to rely too much on research, and they use it as a drunkard uses a lamp post, for support, rather than for illumination.

David Ogilvy, founder of the advertising agency Ogilvy & Mather

Don't get us wrong here: we have nothing against carefully weighing up the risks. We also believe that management tools like strategic planning, competition analysis and market research are absolutely necessary. But – and this is the big but – we should look at the results with a healthy scepticism. Why? Just take a look at the way conventional companies work: Strategic planning is about predicting important developments on the market, planning deployment and distribution of resources, and providing the company with a compass it can steer by in an uncertain world, and all on the basis of certain premises and basic assumptions. Strategies – developed with the help of competition analyses – are based on careful observation of existing competitors and existing products and services. Strategies – developed after close study of the market – are based on tracking the customers' existing preferences.

Rejected by the customer: Red Bull, Post-its and FedEx

So far, so good. But wouldn't it be true to say that these management tools also create an illusion of certainty? Take market research as an example: we know what customers are going to want tomorrow. We've asked them! But were the answers they got from the customers truthful ones?

The customer is a rear view mirror, not a guide to the future.

George Colony, Forrester Research

In fact, customers often have difficulty defining their future needs. That becomes clear when you consider that many innovative products were at first rejected by consumers: Minivans from Chrysler, Post-it notes, video recorders, facsimile machines, Red Bull energy drinks, FedEx overnight delivery, news channel CNN and many others.

So does strategic planning really give us a compass enabling us to steer through the business year ahead? Or is it in fact an illusion that crumbles the minute you take a look through your office window at the real world outside? Does merely observing the competition really give us the competitive edge? Perhaps it does – but then again, perhaps it doesn't. After all, completely new technologies and new and unpredictable rivals that weren't covered by our competition analysis are appearing on the market every day.

Don't be dull. Be daring!

Bill Gates once said:

> Because time has become the competitive factor No 1, you have to be able to hear the grass grow. If you wait for confirmed insights, all you will be able to do is scrabble for the crumbs with the rest of the procrastinators.

If you want to be a business unconventionalist, you can't say, 'Just a moment, we haven't evaluated the results of our 58 market research studies thoroughly enough to make a decision yet.' The examples discussed in this chapter show that you need to be daring to push your company forwards and overtake the competition. And this policy of daring to be different is in stark contrast to those who are swimming with the tide, doing what everyone else is doing and accepting the generally approved rules of behaviour. So be courageous, dare to be different and act now!

Remember: taking tradition into account, scrupulously weighing up the pros and cons and fastidiously gathering and evaluating a profusion of market data all takes time and energy. And it stops you getting on with the really important business!

Out of the box: create completely new markets

In their everyday work, many managers concentrate on their familiar customers, products and services. They devote all their energy to optimizing this field and making minor improvements that give them a temporary edge over their competitors. But it's a hard slog and a bit like being a hamster in a wheel.

The problem is that all their competitors are doing exactly the same thing. The whole industry is fighting over a market that is often already over-saturated. Get out of that hamster wheel! Clever companies do not only operate in their traditional market, but will deliberately cross over into other fields, thus escaping head-on competition.

Rule 4 of business unconventionality

Out of the box: create completely new markets.

Conventional thinking: focus on your existing customers and strive for continual optimization of the products and services you already offer them. This has always worked in the past, so it can't be wrong.

Business unconventionality: escape the typical head-on competition by creating completely new markets. To do so, either develop products and services new to your industry or target completely new customer segments.

One thing needs to be clear from the outset. It takes courage to create new markets: the courage to think unconventional and unorthodox thoughts and the courage to take the risk of losing old customers who are not prepared to follow you on your new path. As French author André Gide put it so aptly, 'One does not discover new continents without consenting to lose sight of the shore.'

The first step towards creating new markets is to subject your existing range of products and services to close scrutiny and to question the traditional target groups for your industry. A radical move, perhaps, but it is precisely this step that makes extremely interesting innovations possible. Aim to create products and services that are new and unusual for your industry, target new customer groups and create new markets.

Another interesting approach is to find an entirely new target group for your existing range, effectively transferring the game to a whole new playing field and outpacing your competitors. The idea behind this clever strategy is not primarily to throw your opponents out of the ring. Instead, business unconventionalists strive to invent games that are played outside the traditional boundaries. That is the essence of unconventional thinking in business. Unless a company is able to think in completely new dimensions, to move beyond what is accepted practice in the industry and dare to be different, it will not be able to shake off the conventional mindset. This is the path to developing new ideas and expanding the classic portfolio to include unusual products and services that customers will love. In other words, your customers remain the same, but what you offer them is new. Let us show you how this strategy can be put into action.

Recreate yourself before you go out of date

Business unconventionalists are always on the lookout, always ready to recognize ongoing changes in the markets. Anyone who is caught napping by new developments will be taught a very hard lesson by those who have kept their eyes open.

As an example, let us take a look at a company whose problem was that slowly but surely its target group was dying out. In such a situation, you can either bewail your fate and, together with your customers, face approaching doom with your head held high – which might be a dignified exit, but wouldn't be very smart – or you can recreate yourself. The company we shall be examining here demonstrates impressively that if you detect signs that your products and services are about to become outdated, you should not despair, but react quickly. If you don't, someone else will do it for you!

US company Arm & Hammer concentrated for many years on the production of baking soda for making bread, cakes and pastries. It was a lucrative business when the firm was founded in 1846. However, baking soda quickly became a standard product with extremely low profit margins, and fewer and fewer US housewives bake. Instead of producing better and better, or cheaper and cheaper, baking soda for a dwindling target group, Arm & Hammer took a close look at the properties of its main product. Apart from baking, what can you use baking soda for? The company discovered three highly interesting facts:

- Baking soda is a natural cleaning agent.
- Baking soda kills odours.
- Baking soda is skin-friendly.

Baking soda is an odour absorber and can therefore be used to neutralize unpleasant smells in refrigerators, laundry baskets and waste bins. It can also be used as a mild cleaning agent for worktops and sinks, and you can even brush your teeth with it. As it is easily digestible and skin-friendly, it can be taken as an antacid or used to treat skin irritations and to refresh tired feet.

Having established this, Arm & Hammer branched out into a completely new field and won over a whole new customer group with innovative cleaning agents and skincare products based on the ingredients of baking soda. Today, it is one of the market leaders in the

Figure 2.1 Baking soda from Arm & Hammer – discovering versatility

Source: Church & Dwight Co Inc, www.armandhammer.com

United States for toothpaste, odour absorbers, deodorants and cleaning and skincare products. All its products are manufactured on the basis of baking soda, its original product. And in its new market, Arm & Hammer was able to successfully differentiate itself from the rest of the field because its products are made using natural ingredients. Of course, it could have set up a subsidiary company to produce the new product lines, but its established name as a producer of baking soda only served to enhance its credibility in the new business area.

Take a look at the world through varifocals

Shifting your perspective in this way offers two fundamental advantages: looking at the world through varifocals enables you to see things both in close-up and from a distance. What does that have to do with business unconventionality? Looking at the world from different perspectives enables a company to stretch the border between the past and the future – to achieve continuous improvement in existing business areas while at the same time investing in the qualitative change that is necessary for the future. The next company we shall be taking a look at follows just such a 'varifocal strategy'. It has continually improved its 'flagship' product, building bricks for children, and simultaneously opened up entirely new markets for the future by offering two innovative services for completely new target groups: family entertainment and management seminars.

The company in question is Danish toy manufacturer LEGO, Europe's largest producer of toys and the world leader in construction toys. Founded in 1932, the company originally made wooden toys. In 1958, it achieved its real breakthrough when it patented the LEGO brick and the corresponding construction system with interlocking plastic building bricks. Each type of LEGO brick is produced in an independent product programme that targets a specific age group.

Playing for new markets: LEGO Serious Play

How did LEGO's varifocal strategy work? The company reacted quickly to attacks by rivals such as Fisher Price and Playmobil, continually updating its products. For example, it introduced the 'Mindstorm Robotics Invention' system where children can build their own robots. In 1997 LEGO computer games were launched, produced under licence. Simultaneously the company strove to win not only the children, but the entire family as customers. This is what the varifocal strategy is about: focusing not only on the immediate target group – children in this case – but looking at wider customer groups – families – in order to create new markets. In 1968, LEGO established its first family fun park, LEGOLAND, one of the biggest tourist attractions in Denmark.

More recently LEGO branched out again, with the opening up of an entirely new market: LEGO for managers. For managers? That doesn't seem to fit in with our picture of top executives. They don't play. Or do they? Well, some of them do seem to be well versed in the game of office politics, but playing with plastic bricks? But it works! There are special LEGO sets for executives. Playing with them, the managers learn to identify problems in the company and find new solutions for them.

Figure 2.2   LEGO Serious Play – playtime for managers

Source: © 2004 The LEGO Group, LEGO, the LEGO logo and SERIOUS PLAY are trademarks of the LEGO Group, here used by special permission

The name of the concept is LEGO Serious Play. Managers play – sorry, work – in groups under the leadership of a specially trained and LEGO-certified trainer. They build metaphors of their organizational experiences with the LEGO bricks. Is their company more a fortress or a racing car? Is the boss a knight on a charger or does he lead from behind the closed doors of his corner office? And when each participant has built a model to represent the characteristics of his or her department, the individual models are joined together to form one unit. In this way, the group gradually creates a complex model of the company structures, revealing common elements and interdependencies, but also problems. This often shows where the weak points in the overall company lie. Many well-known companies have sent their executives to play with LEGO, among them Nokia, Tetra Pak, Varta, Alcatel, Orange and IT systems integrator Comparex.

This example shows how a company can open up completely new markets with clever strategic action, and how a product as mundane as a toy for kids can become a strategic instrument for managers. The bottom line is: If a company can turn children's building blocks into a strategy tool for managers, what's to stop you achieving as much?

Sit up and listen!

Business unconventionalists go through the world with their senses keenly tuned. They look around them, and they know how to listen too. If they didn't, they wouldn't pick up all the invaluable tips to be gleaned from customers, staff and their partners in the market. And business unconventionalists share another outstanding characteristic: they are constantly experimenting and working on recreating their products by asking themselves, 'What will your customers want to buy in future?' 'How can we expand our operations?' and 'Who can we supply with our products and services?' This is what management guru Tom Peters meant when he said:

> Most businessmen think and think and think and plan and plan and plan. They rarely get the point of 'Just do it!' But if we didn't keep trying out new things and creating diversity, we would only have a very limited choice of possibilities to adapt ourselves quickly enough to a rapidly changing world.

So focus not only on today's market, but on the entire potential market of tomorrow, by casting aside conventions and insisting that your colleagues and staff do the same. You, as a business unconventionalist, can get your company ready to outperform the competition.

Revival and reanimation: Barbie fashion

The company in our next example also dared to cast aside conventional ideas. Again, it is a company from the toy industry, this time Mattel. Again, the idea was to win over adults as a new target group. But that's where the similarity ends. This time, it was not a question of targeting managers and focusing on the relevance of the product idea to the business world. The opening Mattel saw was the hopes and dreams of young girls who had now become women – and whom the company decided to reactivate as its customers.

You will probably have guessed that we are talking about Barbie. For decades, millions of little girls all over the world have loved dressing up Barbie and doing her hair. For decades, Mattel have designed new outfits for her, from cocktail dresses to swimwear, business suits, riding outfits and ball gowns. Many of those little girls are now grown up and no longer spend their money on doll's clothes. But Barbie and the image of beauty she incorporates lingers on in their minds.

What better idea, then, than to create a new fashion collection based on the Barbie outfits of the late 1970s – only this time not in doll's size but for the fashion-conscious customer herself? These collections are now sold very successfully in special stores in Japan, and there are plans to sell Barbie fashion at other locations, too.

The interesting thing about this example is that here, a corporation is creating new markets by tapping into the potential target group provided by its former customers. Such a step requires careful planning. It was important to ensure that Mattel's venture into the world of grown-up fashion did not damage or dilute the image of the brand.

Creating new markets on saturated markets

Strategy guru Gary Hamel once said that you must never, ever allow yourself to think that you are in a stagnating industry. There are no stagnating industries, only stagnating managers who are content to pick up on the ideas of others. The example of KBL-Solarien AG, sunbed manufacturers based in Dernbach, Germany, illustrates the truth of this statement. Only 10 years ago, manufacturers of sunbeds had a very comfortable market position. Tanning studios were shooting up everywhere, and they could hardly keep pace with the demand. But the market is saturated now. Hardly any new studios are being opened, existing studios have all the equipment they need, and they have already exhausted the core target group of people who typically visit a tanning studio.

KBL-Solarien, however, was not prepared to simply watch its sales figures dwindle and did not want to engage in price wars with its competitors either. If the present market is saturated, you just have to go out and find yourself a new one!

Identifying not-yet customers

Market analyses revealed that the typical visitors to a tanning studio are young, price-conscious people for whom health risks play only a secondary role. About 8 million people in Germany fall into this category, and this segment had already been targeted. But what about the rest of the population, for example older people for whom the price is not so important, but who are more concerned about the possible health risks? KBL saw enormous potential here. Market research had shown that around 16 million people would be willing to use tanning studios if they were not afraid of the dangers of UV over-exposure. This was a market twice the size of the existing one, which the company intended to keep on catering to. But the best thing of all was that this potential new market was as yet untapped – and wide open for KBL.

The management decided to focus on this new target group. In keeping with the results of the studies, they developed a new-generation sunbed tailored to the requirements of these not-yet customers. The basic idea was that every customer is given a consultation on his or her first visit to the studio, and receives a chip card bearing details of his or her specific skin type, age and other factors. This 'Sun Card' also stores the recommended maximum exposure and the number of minutes spent on the sunbed to date. If there is a danger of over-exposure, the card automatically warns the customer. Parallel to this, KBL also launched a new distribution concept. While hitherto, sunbeds had only been sold to tanning studios, the company now focused its sales efforts on spa hotels, beauty farms and beauty salons. With its special features, the 'Mega Sun' sunbed fitted the concept beautifully, and KBL successfully boosted its growth rates by opening up a whole new market.

'The only limit is your imagination'

This was the advertising slogan for Epson inkjet printers. However, it could also be the motto of the business unconventionalist. There are no limits apart from those imposed by your own imagination. And although nowadays almost everything is imaginable, it is still difficult to shake off the thought patterns of the past.

A good way to break the stranglehold of old established mindsets is to get up off your backside and set out for fresh horizons where you will experience something new. Much of what is changing around you will pass you by if you remain sitting comfortably in your chair. There's too much blocking your view.

Muhammad Yunus did get up and set off to find something new. 'While I was delivering my lectures on economics, people were starving in the villages.' His success story began with this thought, and with a woman in rural Bangladesh who made cane chairs – virtually as a slave to the people who supplied her with the materials. All she needed to free herself from servitude and set up in business on her own was 25 cents. Yunus gave them to her.

Some time later, the professor of economics returned to her village with his students and helped 42 other women with similar problems to set up their own businesses, at a cost of only US$27. This was the beginning of the Grameen Bank – a financial institute set up with the aim of helping women break out of the vicious circle of extortionate interest rates, seizure of their property and resulting poverty by providing them with mini-loans. So far, the bank has helped 2.4 million women in Bangladesh. They repay their loans and the interest punctually and conscientiously, as they know from personal experience that the money is needed to help other women. 'Credit is a fundamental human right,' says Yunus when questioned about his idea, which has turned out to be profitable for both the women and the providers of the capital, and which is now being copied in other developing countries. Business unconventionality at its best!

Passion and the will for change

The lesson is clear: if you settle for the status quo, if you believe you can't change anything, you might as well stop reading right now! Business unconventionalists develop new value creation strategies, and that is not possible without passion and the determination to change things. It is this passion you need as a business unconventionalist, because change is not brought about by organizations, but by dedicated individuals. Or do you think Mahatma Gandhi, Martin Luther King, Nelson Mandela or Václav Havel could have realized their ideas for social change without passion? We are, of course, not suggesting that business unconventionalists' ideas belong in the same category as the achievements of these visionaries, but there are points of comparison. Passionate commitment is the key to all change – and change is exactly what business unconventionality is all about. It is the link between a wish and its fulfilment, between a concept and its realization.

Developing smart ideas for new markets: fun and sport hotel The Cube

Luck or foresight? How are clever and successful ideas for new markets born? The answer: they are always the result of lucky foresight. One thing is clear: no matter how hard you try, you do need the little stroke of luck that will enable you to open up that new market at just the right moment. But to tell you the truth, you can give Lady Luck a nudge in the right direction – by developing a nose for opportunities. Tom Kelley, head of IDEO, a leading design and consulting company specializing in the fields of product development and innovation, says, 'Having a good sense for innovation means being aware of what is happening in the world around you, recognizing trends and being able to react quickly. We cannot afford to wait for a detailed report or until we read about an innovation in a newspaper or on the internet.'

This is precisely the principle of The Cube, an innovative hotel in Austria. Its successful concept is based on the early recognition of trends and consistently catering to the requirements of the target group. In the words of its own advertising, The Cube stands for 'Sleeping, Eating, Relaxing, Chilling, Dancing, Skiing, Snowboarding, Tubing, Biking'. It reaches a whole new target group, hitherto not catered to specifically by traditional hotels: young holidaymakers under 30 looking for entertainment and plenty of sport and leisure activities – but at an affordable price and without the atmosphere of a youth hostel or family boarding house. This sole focus on one specific target group differentiates The Cube from all other hotels in the region.

The Cube has positioned itself as a fun and sport hotel in Nassfeld in Carinthia. The hotel can accommodate up to 646 guests distributed among its 'Cubes', which sleep two, four or eight. 'Distributed' is to be understood literally. At The Cube, you don't book a room. Unless you come as a couple or in groups of four or eight, you won't know until you arrive at the hotel who you will be sharing a 'Cube' with.

There is never a dull moment at The Cube. It advertises 24-hour entertainment and promises its guests a unique experience with indoor and outdoor activities around the clock. The hotel was specially

Figure 2.3 The Cube: dance, chill, ski – and sleep
Source: The Cube Hotels GmbH

designed to suit this concept. Instead of stairs, there are 'Gateways', the guests can take the sports equipment with them to their rooms, there are chill-out zones on every floor, the hotel offers a 24-hour bar, Play Stations and internet terminals, sauna, Turkish bath and ice grotto and an après-sports bar with a sun terrace.

The problem for most hotels in the region is that as ski hotels they are dependent on the winter season. Not so The Cube. It offers nine fun and trendy sport activities: skiing in winter, diving in Lake Pressegger in the summer, plus mountain biking, surfing and much more. In addition, there are events held in the Cube Club, the heart of the hotel's indoor entertainment scene. It offers everything from LAN parties to gaming contests or events with DJs and bands for up to 1,500 party-hungry guests. The owners already plan to copy the concept of The Cube in other locations in Austria and Switzerland.

The key to gaining that competitive edge: first mover

This hotel concept illustrates how business unconventionalists do far more than simply satisfy their customers' basic needs. If you just need a bed to rest your weary body on, you can find that at a youth hostel. But there's more to it than that: The Cube shows that business unconventionalists often *create needs customers didn't even realize they had*, which explains why these companies have customer loyalty ratings and growth rates other firms can only dream of.

Our next example also demonstrates that the key to gaining that competitive edge does not lie in cutting costs, cutting time to market, optimizing resources or improving communication. All these measures are of course vital, but not sufficient by a long way. The true key to gaining a competitive edge is being the first on the market with a new, unusual product or service. A company that can do that can define its customers' expectations for a long time to come – and make a tidy profit into the bargain. The first mover can also make use of valuable resources and partnerships that may be of advantage in the future. The verdict is clear: being the first on the market with a new product, and an unusual product into the bargain, is the best way to be successful.

Built-in coolness factor: Stabilo Boss

An unusual product in the market for ballpoint pens, felt-tips and highlighters? This is a market where price is the decisive factor, and nowadays you can get the basics for school or the office at any discount store. The products have become penny articles produced in the Far East. It's a difficult situation for domestic producers, because you won't hold your own against the cheap discounters simply on the merits of providing better quality.

For Schwan-Stabilo, world market leader for highlighters with its 'Stabilo Boss', it was clear that new strategies were needed. The company, based in Heroldsberg, Germany, was well aware that it needed to solve this problem – and do it fast.

So it turned its attention to an interesting target group, the 12- to 19-year-olds for whom it is not only important that the product performs its basic function – writing on paper – but who are primarily looking for a product that stands out from the rest – a product with a built-in coolness factor.

It was above all the coolness factor that enabled the company to be so successful in the market. Schwan-Stabilo had always been a traditional company – it is a family-owned business founded in 1855. But its advantage was that its competitors in the Far East lacked direct access to the target group in question and were hardly likely to spend money on in-depth trend research.

So in order to develop trendy, cool pens and markers for this target group, Schwan-Stabilo focuses not only on functionality, but also on design and marketing aspects. The company employs trend scouts who report back on the latest developments within the target group. This led, for example, to the development of a highlighter with a tattoo print , and the 's'move', which comes equipped with a basketball cover.

At Schwan-Stabilo, a research team of 20 works on new product development. There is a demand for new ergonomic shapes, special spring-loaded nibs, non-smudging gel-rollers, and so the company has consciously positioned its range as high-tech products. At the same time, it produces a stream of innovative new ideas for products that customers may not in fact actually need, but which nevertheless sell well because they are trendy, colourful and stylish. For example, there is a range of 'mini' highlighters, ink rollerball pens in new colours mirroring the latest trends in fashion and cosmetics, and the 'Woody', which is available in two sizes and is a coloured pencil, a water paint and a wax crayon all rolled into one. This product is especially popular with kids.

Figure 2.4 Pens with a built-in coolness factor from Schwan-Stabilo
Source: Schwan-STABILO, Schwanhäusser GmbH & Co KG

The company also aimed for an image transfer. To improve brand perception with younger people, Schwan-Stabilo now sponsors snowboarding and music events. Online marketing and a trendy, dynamic internet presence round off the new alignment of the company. The concept is working: in contrast to the general trend in the industry, Stabilo is seeing positive growth figures. According to the trade association of the German paper, office supplies and stationery industry, Germans are spending less and less money on writing materials, but Stabilo has boosted its turnover.

Inventing new business models: Dell Computer

We said above that the key to gaining that competitive edge lies in being first on the market with a new, unusual, pioneering product or service. There is one other thing, though: you can also get the edge over your competitors by being the first to launch a new, pioneering business model. So business unconventionalists don't only innovate in the field of their products and services, but look much further than that. They also take a good hard look at their business model. Real business unconventionalists can find totally new concepts or totally new ways in which to ensure that their business model clearly differentiates them from the rest. And while the others are busy thinking up new ways to cut costs and lower prices in order to grab a larger piece of the market, business unconventionalists are focusing their attention somewhere else entirely, and are developing whole new business models where there is real money to be made.

Michael Dell is just such a business unconventionalist. He reinvented the business concept for computer manufacturers and thus became one of the most successful (and richest) businesspeople in the United States. Dell's business model differs from the conventional model of the PC industry in three ways:

- First, Dell sells its products exclusively to the end user, cutting intermediaries, retailers and systems integrators out of the picture completely.
- Second, the end user gets a truly tailor-made product, a computer that is screwed together – sorry, configured – to conform 100 per cent to his or her specific wishes and requirements, and not a ready-configured product sold by some computer store that thinks it knows what's good for the customer.

- The third point where Dell's concept differs from the conventional business model for the industry lies in the coordination mechanism for the production of the computers. The industry norm is to pre-produce computers in accordance with the latest sales prognoses, thus generating warehousing costs. Dell, however, produces each computer to order. And this is the really clever part of it: Dell, however, produces a computer especially for you and uses your money to do it! Warehousing costs are kept to a minimum, the latest technology can be incorporated, and the cash flow is positive and straight to the manufacturer. The customers profit, too. They get a customized product at a relatively low price. And this, in turn, gives Dell an enormous competitive edge.

Start early – and with passion

We have seen that the founder of the company, Michael Dell, not only came up with a completely new business model for the industry, but was also the first in the PC-industry to come up with the revolutionary new idea of mass customization. So is Michael Dell someone who has the words 'business unconventionalist' tattooed across his forehead? Well, no matter how many interviews with or reports on him you read, the words that immediately come to mind to describe him are smart but boring. Which just goes to prove our theory that there is no stereotype for the business unconventionalist. You don't have to be an extremely extroverted person or a PR-hungry egomaniac to make history with unconventional ideas.

And yet there is one thing that all business unconventionalists have in common, and that is *passion*. In the case of Michael Dell, it was a passion for figures and technology that was noticeable at a very early age. There is an anecdote about this, which was told by Barry Gibbons in his outstanding book *Dream Merchants and HowBoys*. Michael's parents gave him a personal computer for his 15th birthday, and as though he somehow knew that he was destined to become a legend, Michael took the computer to his room and took it apart. The fact that he stripped it right down to its individual components is probably not the stuff that legends are made of, but the amazing thing is that he was only 15 years old and that he put it back together again and it worked.

Our next business unconventionalist is a completely different type of person. Guy la Liberté began his career as a street performer earning his money as a fire-eater. Later he founded Canadian Cirque du Soleil, nowadays a global entertainment empire that has redefined the conventional circus industry. The Cirque du Soleil has a circus ring and a circus tent, but that's about all it has in common with the traditional circus as we know it. The Cirque du Soleil offers a mixture of musical and performance: a show rather than a circus. There are no animals – no dancing bears, no lions or elephants – and all the acts are linked, by a storyline.

Business unconventionality in perfection: Cirque du Soleil

The Cirque du Soleil takes its audience on a journey through emotional dream worlds with dance, song, theatre and performing artistes. It's an unforgettable experience that people are willing to pay a little more for. The concept is very well thought out. Because it has no performing animals, the Cirque is able to reduce costs. It also has no orchestra. Instead, it invests in lighting and sound – and, of course, in the performers. Some of the artistes are former top athletes, for example from the field of rhythmic or apparatus gymnastics; others are trained musical actors. The Cirque du Soleil employs scouts who are always on the lookout for new talents – they establish contacts with athletes at the Olympic Games, for example. Athletes from the former Eastern Bloc or China, in particular, are attracted by the good money to be earned at the Cirque du Soleil.

All this keeps costs very low for the Cirque du Soleil, as everything it needs is readily available anywhere in the world. This provides optimum conditions for the company's real stroke of genius: multiplication. Each show is produced as a whole from beginning to end. Several ensembles rehearse the same show and then tour all over the world with it. One and the same show runs in several locations simultaneously, and one choreographed routine is used for three to five years.

Tickets cost between €50 and €100. In this way, the company focuses on a more upmarket target group. And the Cirque du Soleil doesn't only earn money from the box-office takings: in the intervals there are stands, and a large share of the revenue comes from the sale of merchandising goods sold there, for example T-shirts, coffee mugs, CDs and DVDs.

Founded in 1984, the company now operates globally and has skilfully carved out a niche for itself and created a totally new market by
combining various popular forms of entertainment: assembly-line
produced flights of fantasy for a clientele that is prepared to dig deep
into their pockets!

Courage, perseverance, vision: the tools of business unconventionality

We said at the beginning of this chapter that the mark of a business
unconventionalist is the courage to dare to break the established rules
of the industry, and by now you will have a pretty good idea what we
meant: Michael Dell and Guy la Liberté, and also Ingvar Kamprad of
Ikea, are totally different personalities, but they share a few important
characteristics. They have all shown courage and perseverance. And
they all have a vision – and we are not talking about the corporate
visions that are dreamed up behind boardroom doors by well-paid
executives and consultants and in the end are nothing more than interchangeable, hollow self-adulation. When we say vision, we mean what
humanistic philosopher and psychologist Erich Fromm described so
aptly: if life has no vision, with no ultimate goal towards which we
strive, no single objective to fulfil, there is no point in making an effort.

Herman Mashaba had such a vision – 'a dream that would
strengthen the hearts and the souls of my black fellow countrymen, a
dream that would make them beautiful, proud and strong'.

It was in order to make this vision reality that he founded his
company Black like Me in the South African town of Garankuwa,
north of Pretoria, in 1985. Against all opposition from the South
African apartheid regime, he and his staff of four began to produce
handmade shampoos and soaps for a clearly defined target group:
the black population of South Africa. And with unbelievable
courage, perseverance and commitment, he created a profitable
cosmetics company which is today in the process of expanding onto
international markets.

Business unconventionality box

Recreate yourself before you go out of date!

Escape the typical head-to-head competition by creating totally new markets. Develop products and services that are unconventional for your industry or conquer completely new customer segments!

Remember Danish toy manufacturer LEGO, which opened up an entire new market parallel to its traditional market (children's toys): it launched LEGO Serious Play, a building bricks set for managers. Or think of KBL-Solarien: when it had exhausted its customary customer group – tanned and fitness-studio-honed wearers of gold jewellery – it identified a whole new market which offered tremendous potential. This consisted of health-conscious consumers who had so far avoided the tanning studio because of the risk of UV over-exposure.

The example of companies such as the Grameen Bank in Bangladesh and Black like Me in South Africa prove that this strategy is not only effective on the markets of the industrialized nations.

Maxi size and mini size: place no geographical limits on your success

Please don't expect an eloquent treatise on globalization, on the elimination of geographical borders or the increasing economic importance of the so-called threshold nations such as India or Vietnam. Numerous books have been written on this subject, it has been discussed in even more television programmes, and it is not what we are talking about here. Globalization is here. It is a fact and no matter how many demonstrators raise their voices against it, it is here to stay, a development that they will neither stop nor reverse.

The interesting question that we will be dealing with in this section is an entirely different one. How can you swim against the tide, against the trend in your industry, and still be very successful, either locally or globally?

Local, regional, global

Take a look at your industry. Many companies place artificial limitations upon themselves by supplying only regional markets. But why? We talk of a mobile society, expect our staff to be geographically mobile – but why don't we show our potential customers just how flexible we can be?

On the other hand, there are industries where global commitment is a precondition for success, where the small fry don't stand a chance. Or do they? It is possible to become a 'local hero' by deliberately going against the trend and successfully occupying a regional niche despite the multinational groups! But it takes courage.

Rule 5 of business unconventionality

Maxi size and mini size: place no geographical limits on your success.

Conventional thinking: you respect the geographical borders of your industry. For example, if your industry centres exclusively on a regional alignment, you tailor your products and services to the requirements of local customers.

Business unconventionality: you deliberately set out to swim against the geographical alignment of your industry and create your own economic boost.

In most industries there are geographical borders, that are more or less strictly adhered to. As a rule and for the majority of companies, development always moves in one direction – towards the bigger and the more international. Industries that hitherto operated predominantly locally (such as retail companies) are becoming more international. Industries that operated predominantly nationally (such as airlines) are striving to become global players. The potential for business unconventionalists in this situation lies in questioning these developments and if necessary, doing exactly the opposite.

Two examples may help. While undertakers usually operate regionally, Service Corporation International (SCI) is a stock-exchange listed, vertically integrated global player. It ignored the predominantly regional alignment of the industry and became a globally operating service company. SCI has almost 2,500 business locations worldwide, including 451 cemeteries and 189 crematoria.

In contrast, think of the many microbreweries. While the general development in the brewery industry is from regional to international brewery groups, tiny local microbreweries are experiencing a comeback in many areas.

How can you successfully defy the geographical limits of your industry?

An international cult: 8,500 Starbucks coffee shops

The success of Starbucks shows that you can change the landscape of your industry, even if you start from modest beginnings. The story began with a chain of four shops in Seattle, selling coffee, tea and spices. The founder of Starbucks had discovered a market niche, but not exploited its full potential. In a country where the coffee usually fails to meet the expectations of the pampered Middle European palate (and that's putting it nicely), Starbucks coffee was a real exception to the rule. It seems the state of Washington, in the north-west of the United States, is not only a Mecca for computer enthusiasts, aircraft fans and lovers of grunge music, but also the home of people who appreciate good coffee.

So the company already had a good product. That's a good basis, but not nearly enough to guarantee the kind of international success Starbucks enjoys today. And that's where a true business unconventionalist enters the story! You will remember that a business unconventionalist is someone with courage and a vision. We have already seen that Michael Dell and Guy la Liberté possess both these qualities. And so does another business unconventialist and innovator. His name: Howard Schultz. His function: retail and marketing manager with an ambition for higher things. Starbucks brings people together. It is a sort of piazza, a 'third place' after home and work, an Acropolis of the 21st century where the focus is on the product as well as on the experience. Wow! That's a vision that really deserves the name! The only question is, why hadn't anybody else thought of it? But that's a different story.

Back to the coffee shop in rainy Seattle. Business was only moderately successful until Howard Schulz took over the chain, which by now comprised several shops. He resolutely threw the spices out of the product range and focused on the coffee experience, setting Starbucks on the road to unparalleled expansion. Today, the company has more than 8,500 branches all over the world, with more coffee bars being added each day. There is no sign of an end to its global expansion, and the company's declared target of 20,000 branches can only be achieved through a dominant presence on every continent. This means that in future, there will be a new word for 'coffee' in Asia, Europe, Africa, Australia and South America, too.

Going against the established culture: Café Sacher versus Starbucks

To attract as many customers as possible, Starbucks deliberately looks for locations on busy street corners and on the ground floors of large office complexes. Schultz will open a new Starbucks store in the direct vicinity of or even opposite an existing one. This means customers don't have to wait in peak trading hours, and leaves less room for Starbucks' competitors to move into the area. Starbucks can design, fit out and open a new store in just a few weeks.

In Vienna, Starbucks has even ventured to open a store right opposite the famous Café Sacher. Sacrilege in the home of coffee house culture! In Vienna, the Kaffeehaus is an institution where time seems to stand still. Distinguished local notaries have their own special tables reserved for them, and guests are welcomed and served with old-fashioned courtesy. Otto Friedländer once said, 'For the Viennese, the Kaffeehaus is an extension of their living rooms', which sums it all up. The Viennese are at home in their Kaffeehaus. There, they can enjoy their coffee, read the newspapers, meet friends, play chess and be alone without feeling alone. And so it was hardly surprising that the news that a Starbucks was opening prompted newspaper columnists to foresee a threat to the Viennese Kaffeehaus tradition. In reality, though, Starbucks is hardly a threat. The target groups are too different, and so the Kaffeehaus and Starbucks live in peaceful coexistence.

There is, however, one critical question that arises here. Why didn't any of the traditional firms come up with the idea of extending their geographical limits? If the Starbucks chain now has more than 8,500 branches worldwide, what might the legendary Café Sacher, with its history and the magic of its famous name, have achieved? But stop! Sacher recognized the signs of the times and has now embarked on a course of – albeit modest – expansion – and compared to Starbucks' ambitious growth this seems like a drop in the ocean. Sacher has opened branches in Salzburg, Innsbruck and Graz.

Local heroes: microbreweries

Just take a look at the brewery industry. It is dominated by global players such as Heineken and Carlsberg, yet on a regional level there are numerous small breweries which have proved that it is possible to carve out a niche for yourself in an increasingly globalized market.

In Basel, Switzerland, two local pioneering breweries dominate the scene: Fischerstube with its Ueli-Bier, and the Unser Bier brewery, provide fine beers brewed in the region. Ueli-Bier is made in Kleinbasel, in the Rheingasse, and Unser Bier in Grossbasel in the Laufenstrasse. Of course, we are talking quality, not quantity here: together, they brew only about 7,000 hectolitres per year. As a comparison, global leader Anheuser-Busch has an annual production of 147 million hectolitres.

Such small specialized breweries in a market of giants can be extremely successful. In Germany, highly profitable, local, medium-sized breweries like Augustiner in Munich, the Gaffel Becker private brewery in Cologne and Peter Frankenheim in Düsseldorf, which brews the famous Altbier, demonstrate that there is money to be made, even in tough times, if you can find a lucrative niche in the market.

Think anti-trend: for example organic

Think against the prevailing trends! Many of the most promising gaps in the market are to be found in the counter-trends rather than among the mainstream products and services. As soon as there are signs that the market in a particular segment or for a particular type of product is about to go stale, it's time to jump onto the pendulum as it swings the other way. The general trend is towards increasing internationalization. The counter-trend: go local!

Feneberg Lebensmittel GmbH in Germany takes the motto 'from here' very literally. In mid-1998 it launched its range of organically produced foods: fruit and vegetables, beef, eggs, dairy produce, cheeses, bread and cakes, from the region and for the region. Feneberg markets its products under the slogan 'From here: quality from A to Z.'

The company deliberately set out to offer an alternative to the increasing globalization of commodity flows in the food industry. It offers consumers the chance to support the economic stability of their region by choosing to buy vegetables grown locally instead of those from Spain, Holland or Israel. The advantages of this home-grown organic produce are obvious. 'From here' products mean:

- absolutely fresh produce that has not been transported over long distances (it is produced within a radius of 100 km around the town of Kempten);
- cost-saving through direct delivery;
- greater consumer confidence in products they know are produced locally;
- a contribution towards preserving the cultural landscape and the environment;
- support for local agriculture.

Feneberg's partners are farmers from the region of Allgäu/Swabia, and are all members of an approved organic farming association. They are subject to strict regulation, and their produce is either processed by Feneberg's own facilities or by other regional plants – also in strict adherence to the principles of organic production.

The feel-good factor: organic produce delivered to your door

Feneberg does not convince consumers with the quality of its products alone, but also with its stores, which it refers to as 'Feel-good markets'. Starting at the beginning of the 1980s, it analysed customer requirements and redesigned all its stores accordingly. The aisles are wide enough to allow plenty of room for the customers and their shopping trolleys. The goods are arranged systematically according to product group, and Feneberg attaches great importance to providing a friendly atmosphere. All these aspects have made Feneberg a successful regional brand that has no problem holding its own against the big supermarket chains.

The organic farm Adamah in Markgrafneusiedl in Austria takes this concept one step further. Adamah found that consumers don't necessarily want to buy vegetables from Holland, Spain or Chile in the impersonal atmosphere of a supermarket. Many people are prepared to pay a higher price for quality products which are locally produced, bypassing the supermarkets altogether.

Adamah set out to cater to this trend. It has a regular home delivery service supplying its customers with organically grown fruit and vegetables of the season, produce that has not been transported over long distances and is therefore really fresh, not to mention the other advantages already listed for Feneberg. Adamah, however, has one added advantage for consumers: they save time they would otherwise spend shopping.

Customers identify themselves with the product: reinventing the local newspaper

Going regional is also a counter-trend that can be seen in the print media industry. While more and more newspaper companies are merging and the market for daily newspapers is increasingly dominated by just a handful of national and international media corporations, regional dailies such as *Vorarlberger Nachrichten* from Austria have found their niche. Such regional companies know that they cannot compete with the national newspapers and therefore need to create a profile that is distinctive by specializing above all in local news. *Vorarlberger Nachrichten*, for example, sees itself not merely as a regional newspaper carrying local ads, but also as a portal via which its subscribers can take advantage of excellent deals made with telecommunication providers, utility companies and other regional suppliers.

The man behind the success of *Vorarlberger Nachrichten* is 'publishing guru' Eugen A Russ. His concept for a successful regional paper is more tabloid-style news, more sport and above all, giving the consumers real value for their money. Subscribers should be able to save more money by benefiting from excellent deals with telecommunication providers and other companies than the subscription costs them.

The concept goes even further than that. The idea is that a local paper is only a good paper if all readers find a picture of themselves and their friends in it at least once a year. Therefore, Russ has reporters with cameras and microphones touring the region and reporting on private parties. One of the advantages is that this gives *Vorarlberger Nachrichten* a photo databank in which almost one in three inhabitants of the region is featured. As not every photo makes it into the paper, the stories are continued on the web portal (www.vol.at), where every reader is free to become involved interactively. The aim is to create an active community that shows readers, 'Your local paper is there for you!'

Russ didn't create this concept entirely on his own. It's an idea he picked up while travelling through the United States, and one which has been copied several times. This, however, isn't a problem: local heroes seldom get in each other's way!

This trend towards regionalization reflects one of the consumer's basic needs today. In an increasingly complex world, people are looking for something they can identify with, the reassurance of the familiar. Regionalization is thus a symbolic framework that smart businesses can fill with meaning.

Whether you aim to be a global player or a local hero, you will have to answer one fundamental question: how can you ensure that consumers will buy your products and services rather than those of your competitors? Starbucks has found its answer: It's not just the product, it's more than the location – it's a philosophy that permeates every aspect of the business. 'We're not in the coffee business serving people – we're in the people business serving coffee.'

And now some homework for you: Replace the word 'coffee' with the name of your product, and you will have an interesting concept that ought to set you thinking!

Business unconventionality box

Do not simply follow the trends! Many of the most interesting opportunities on the market are to be found in the counter-trends rather than in the mainstream.

Think about it: How can you swim against the tide – and against the current trends in your industry – do business successfully, either locally or globally?

Remember SCI, the undertakers that came up with a revolutionary innovation for what is a very regional business. Or think of the coffee bars, which traditionally operate regionally. The innovator comes from Seattle: It started out with just four coffee bars, but today Starbucks has more than 8,500 branches all over the world. But also remember the example of the microbreweries, which move in the opposite direction. They deliberately eschew global expansion strategies and concentrate instead on becoming the number one in their local market.

Mix it! Conquer new markets with innovative combinations

In his book *Thinking About Management*, published in 1991, Harvard economist Theodore Levitt writes:

> Differentiating yourself from the rest of the field is one of the most important strategic and tactical challenges a company faces constantly. It's not a judgement call .... There are in fact no standardized, inter-changeable products, only people who think and act like that.

Before you nod in agreement, we have to ask you one question. If everyone agrees that the only way to remain competitive over the long term is to clearly stand out from the rest of the field, then why is it that so few companies have a good answer to the question, 'What makes you unique? In what way are you different from your competitors?'

We asked this question recently at a workshop held for a bank. The answer we got was: 'Quality, innovation and customer service'. Sorry, but that's not going to win you any accolades on today's tough markets. All your competitors would give us exactly the same answer. In other words, quality, innovation and customer service are a matter of course today. They are nothing exceptional and are not enough to make you stand out from the rest of the field. They won't give your company a distinctive profile.

Mix and match

In this section we shall be taking a look at how you – as a true business unconventionalist – can make sure your company stands out from the rest of the field. We would like to introduce you to an interesting concept: the concept of mixing and matching. It's a simple but effective approach which combines products and services in a new way. And the crazier the combination, the more unique the mix will be!

Rule 6 of business unconventionality

Mix it! Conquer new markets with innovative combinations.

Conventional thinking: expand your existing range by simply adding products and services that are already familiar and standard for your industry.

Business unconventionality: combine products and services from two different industries to offer a completely new mix. This simple but effective approach consists in linking products and services in a new way. And the crazier the mix, the more unique the combination will be!

Of course, in every industry there are unwritten rules governing how business is done. For example, you get legal advice in a lawyer's office and not at the airport or in a coffee bar. Why should that be so? Why are there these 'sacred cows' in every industry? Usually simply because that's the way it's always been done. But don't forget, sacred cows can be turned into very juicy steaks!

Coffee and counsel: divorce US-style

A law office in a coffee shop: this business model is a real innovation offered by lawyer Jeffrey J Hughes in Los Angeles. The days when clients had to come to his office to get legal advice are long gone. Today, clients can consult their lawyer in the relaxed atmosphere of a coffee shop – and for an unbeatably low fee into the bargain. A simple consultation, which lasts between 15 and 30 minutes depending on the case, costs just US$25 – and the coffee is included in the price. Just like at McDonald's, there is a list on the wall showing the charge for different services: change of name US$200, entry on the trade register US$500, and so on. There are now around 30 lawyers working according to this system. There are experts on family law, labour law and tenancy law, on immigration, taxation, accidents, suing for damages and insolvency. 'It's something completely different. You meet in pleasant surroundings where people are much more relaxed than they would be in an office. And I find new clients there,' says Keith J Simpson, a specialist in family law who offers his services at 'Coffee & Counsel' for two hours twice a week.

All the lawyers participating in the scheme are serious representatives of their profession. The café functions as a place of initial contact with a relaxed atmosphere that helps people overcome their hesitation to take legal advice, particularly as the fee for the first consultation is so low.

Logical combinations: the bookstore with cookery books – and something to eat

Babette's is a bookstore in Vienna that specializes in cookery books and is located near the famous Naschmarkt food market. It also sells exotic spices. Nothing special, you might think. But Babette's is a typical mix-and-match combination. The store stocks more than a thousand cookery books and also offers something to eat. It is a bookshop, spice store and demonstration kitchen all rolled into one, and offers its guest a different menu every day. Cookery courses and culinary events are also held on the premises.

The people behind Babette's – to be found both behind the counter and in front of the stove – are Nathalie Pernstich and Silke Huala, two businesswomen, cooks, artists and bibliophiles. And above all, they are two women who enjoy good food. The idea for Babette's arose out of their love of cooking, of books, of spices and of good food as an expression of the enjoyment of life. And out of their conviction that

Figure 2.5   Cooking for bookworms – Babette's in Vienna
Source: Babette's

Vienna, with its many hobby chefs and Naschmarkt fans, had long deserved a store like it.

By the way, neither of them is a professional chef or a professional bookseller. Nathalie Pernstich is a qualified IT consultant and worked in the telecommunications field, while Silke Huala studied painting and trained as an art teacher. Perhaps it was the fact that they came from other fields that enabled them to come up with such an innovative combination.

My beautiful launderette

'Make waiting for your laundry more enjoyable' is the concept behind the 'Cleanicum' on the Brüsseler Platz in Cologne. The Cleanicum is not only a launderette, but also a lounge. Cologne's inner city area offers plenty of customers looking for somewhere to do their washing: rents are high, and apartments are small, with little space for a washing machine. The problem: More 'upmarket' customers were not attracted to the typical launderette concept. After all, you spend some time there waiting until your laundry is washed and then dried, and the atmosphere in a conventional launderette is far from inviting. The people behind the Cleanicum realized this and came up with a concept for a launderette where getting your laundry done is more of an added bonus. People meet there, relax on cosy loungers, can surf the internet and, of course, have an espresso. They can read if they're looking for peace and quiet. Sometimes people even fall asleep waiting for their laundry to finish its cycle – which the owners see as a sign that they feel especially at home and comfortable there.

And that's exactly how the Cleanicum wants its customers to feel: pampered, which is why special attention is paid to the service. Sometimes the launderette becomes a support centre, where the staff help customers with small errands or customers offer each other advice on all kinds of subjects. Rumour has it that some have even found their partner for life there.

Business in the third place: Art bar & café

As we have already seen, legal consultations in a café are already a reality, at least in the United States. And now the insurance industry is also discovering that it does more business when it presents its services to potential new customers in more relaxed surroundings than an

Figure 2.6 One of the cleanest addresses in Germany – the 'in-crowd'
meets at the Cleanicum
Source: Cleanicum OHG

insurance company's offices. In so-called 'third places' – places
between the home and the workplace – insurance policies are offered
as a sort of additional extra, thus reaching completely new target
groups. The Munich Hiscox Art Bar & Restaurant has positioned
itself less as an insurance office and more as a place where people
meet to enjoy art and the pleasures of life, as an attractive third place.
The model for the Munich establishment is British insurance giant
Hiscox's Art Café in London, which has become a platform for the
British art scene. Hiscox doesn't only insure art, the company lives it,
as a PR text says. In the German branch, customers can enjoy meals,
buy works of art and see for themselves the truth of the insurance
company's motto, as formulated by board member Joachim Leuth:
'We insure the good things in life.'

Even more interesting combinations: Figaro's innovations

Mix- and-match business models combining elements from very
different industries have also been set up in the hairdressing trade:

- Salon Kaiserschnitt in Berlin-Friedrichshain offers a combination of a hairdressing salon and a home fashion store. The interior decoration of the store is also for sale.
- There are many more examples of a combination of a hairdressing salon and a café. A hairstylist and a French confectioner share the premises of the Salon Sucre in Berlin-Kreuzberg. And the café-bistro Redetzky's in Berlin has opened a new branch in the Cutman hairdressing salon.
- In his salons in Hamburg, Berlin and Munich, Gerhard Meir focuses on print media. The existing selection of magazines for browsing is soon to be joined by a library, inviting customers to linger and making their visit even more enjoyable.

All these examples show that there's no limit to the possibilities of the mix-it concept, apart from the limits of your imagination.

More than the sum of its parts: Library Hotel

Which mix-it concepts work best? Those where the value of the whole is more than the sum of its parts. In other words, a successful mix-and-match concept is one where the elements are combined in such a way that added value is created.

One example of this principle is the Library Hotel in New York. In a city where there is no lack of unusual hotel concepts, the Library Hotel still manages to attract attention. The hotel, situated on Madison Avenue, corner of 41st Street, is the first of its kind. Everything revolves around reading. Each floor of this luxury establishment is devoted to a different subject, and the rooms on that floor are equipped with books and works of art dealing with that particular subject. Altogether, the management of the hotel has purchased some 6,000 books and distributed them among the 60 rooms. To enable guests to find their rooms more easily, each of the hotel's 12 floors is dedicated to a different area of interest, much as the sections in a library are labelled: social sciences, languages, mathematics and natural sciences, technology, the arts, literature, history, general knowledge, philosophy and religion. And each individual room on that floor contains books on a different aspect of this subject.

Figure 2.7 The Library Hotel proves it – a symbiosis is the combination of two systems to mutual advantage
Source: The Library Hotel, www.libraryhotel.com

Guests will not only find reading matter in their hotel room and in the lobby. There is also a mahogany-panelled reading room which invites them to browse, a cosy conservatory ('Poetry Garden') under the roof, the 'Writer's Den' with wing armchairs and an open fireplace, and the breakfast room, which offers floor-to-ceiling bookshelves and a selection of newspapers. All day, guests can eat, drink – and of course read – there.

The owner, Henry Kallan, had the idea for the Library Hotel when, shortly after acquiring the 12-storey building, which he intended to convert into a hotel, he took a walk through the neighbouring streets and passed first the New York Public Library and then, just a few blocks away, the Pierpont Morgan Library. The idea was so successful that rooms at the Library Hotel now cost between US$315 and US$800 per night.

This example shows how successful the mix-and-match concept can be when it is skilfully applied. We live in a society where everything we can possibly imagine is available in abundance. The natural reaction is to look for something that is just a little bit different. Something that stands out from the rest, something unexpected. And that is exactly what you are creating when you mix and match! The crazier the combination, the more unique the result will be – and the more attractive to the customer.

Business unconventionality box

The most successful concepts are frequently combinations of existing ideas.

Jason Jennings, business consultant and author

Why don't you put together ideas from two different industries and create a new business model? The idea is, of course, not simply to mix any ideas from two different industries but to create a unique product or service mix with a clear strategic aim and your current (or potential) target group in mind, a product or service mix that represents added value for the customer. Combine ideas from two different industries to create a completely new mix. This is a simple but very successful approach in which existing ideas are combined in a new way. And the crazier the combination, the more unique the result will be!

Remember the Library Hotel in New York, which found a way to stand out from the rest by creating a combination of a library and a hotel. Or the concept of US lawyer Jeffrey J Hughes, who combined his lawyer's offices with a coffee shop. Another attractive example comes from the otherwise unexciting launderette scene. The Cleanicum in Cologne combined a launderette with a trendy lounge – under the motto 'Make waiting for your laundry more enjoyable'.

Quasi-monopolies: be the champion; create a temporary monopoly in your market

The business pages of our newspapers are full of reports on spectacular mergers. The advantages seem obvious: synergies mean that costs can be cut, the value of a company and its yield increase, product ranges complement each other. That's the theory. However, the majority of mergers fail to produce the desired effect. Indeed, a study by investment bankers Morgan Stanley revealed that 70 per cent of mergers are unsuccessful. And yet the 'big is beautiful' trend continues seemingly unabated. Of course, the idea of putting two and two together and making five does have its charms: as the CEO of the business empire created by such a merger, you can make impressive speeches, meet important people, smoke expensive cigars and drink cognac while the bosses of smaller companies are left out in the cold.

Rule 7 of business unconventionality

Quasi-monopolies: be the champion; create a temporary monopoly in your market.

Conventional thinking: Following the principle of spreading risks, you create a wide portfolio of products and services hoping to counter-balance a weak performance in one area through good performance in others.
Business unconventionality: Be bold, find a niche or carve one out for yourself. Create your own temporary monopoly.

As long as competition was limited to a regional level, the policy of acquisitions and mergers at all costs worked well, and many mega corporations in the emerging economies are still very successful on their protected domestic markets today. An example is India's Tata group, the largest business group in the country, with operations extending into all areas of life. The activities of this biggest private group enterprise in India span such widely varying operations as the manufacture of cars and trucks, the supply of electricity, internet services, consulting, luxury hotels, tea plantations, computer and IT services and the production of clocks and watches. However, in the highly industrialized economies of Western Europe or North America, this concept no longer works as well.

The times they are a-changin': small is beautiful

The days of huge, widely diversified business groups are numbered. In the age of surplus, companies need clear-cut profiles. And so it is vital not to aim for size at all costs, but to focus on those areas of business where you have a competitive edge over your competitors.

You must find the right niches for your company, the niches where your company really is world-class, and concentrate on them. To do this effectively, you must develop a range of products or services tailored precisely to the requirements of a clearly defined target group, and – very important – you must be able to deliver the goods on a regular basis. In his book *Hidden Champions*, Hermann Simon outlines two different concepts for carving out a niche:

> In the first category, there are the true specialists who aim to establish a strong market position in very small markets ('Be very big in small markets'). I call them the Super-Nichists. The companies in the other category create their own markets. They have no competitors in the conventional sense. I call them market owners, as they practically own the markets they operate in.

Here are two striking examples. Swedish company Bergman & Beving, with a staff of only 85, holds a comfortable global market share of 50 per cent with a product most of us will have had in our mouths at some time or another: the saliva remover used by dentists. And Rational AG, based in Landsberg am Lech in Bavaria, has just one product in its portfolio and has been global market leader for years with it: a steam cooking system for hotel, restaurant and canteen kitchens.

Business unconventionalists as experts – experts as business unconventionalists

If you asked Manfred Utsch where his company's strengths lie, he would answer, 'We are the global leader in car registration systems.'

As the leading producer of car number plates, Manfred Utsch's medium-sized enterprise is a showcase company for a world-class niche player. Customers from 100 different countries buy car number plates and registration systems from the company based in the German city of Siegen.

For example, Utsch has developed special laser and hologram techniques for use in countries with high car theft rates. In Sri Lanka, cars have two number plates and an additional sticker that is attached to the inside of the windscreen. The sticker automatically self-destructs if any attempt is made to remove it from the windscreen.

Utsch is successful because it is occupying a niche on the market and it has made the most of that niche. While the company originally only produced conventional number plates, it later began to sell machinery, and now sells its production equipment to manufacturers of car registration plates all over the world, thus also boosting its servicing and spare parts divisions.

But Utsch does more than that. The company invests in new development, researches new technologies and has long since transformed itself from a mere manufacturer of vehicle number plates to the world's leading expert on number plates and registration systems. Utsch even advises governments on the introduction of new registration plates, and now successfully licenses its technology to other companies. Yet despite this expansion, Utsch has remained loyal to its niche. It has increased its range of products and services to fill that niche, but never squandered its energy by straying too far from its core competencies.

Niches for down-to-earth products: Josef Z and his unusual chocolate bars

A bar of Ritter Sport chocolate costs €0.69 – even less when it's on special offer. A bar of Zotter chocolate weighing only 70 grammes costs on average €2.70. But this is no ordinary chocolate in common-or-garden flavours like 'fruit and nut' or 'dairy milk'. Zotter chocolate comes in varieties such as 'lemon and polenta' or 'crushed pepper with mint oil', and is hand-scooped. Josef Zotter, the chocolatier from Styria in Austria, is very inventive and has created a super-niche for his company with highly unusual and sometimes quite daring combinations, for example 'hempseed and mocha' or 'coffee plums with caramelized bacon'.

His business model stands out from that of other companies on the confectionery market today in many important aspects. Zotter uses no artificial colouring, flavouring or preservatives, and ingredients of only the highest quality. And because quality has its price, Zotter does not participate in the price wars that have been raging in the retail trade for many years now – and is nevertheless successful. The company sells 2 million bars of its hand-scooped chocolate a year, and that despite the fact that a bar of Zotter chocolate costs over three times more than a bar of ordinary chocolate.

The company's sales network also differs from that of traditional chocolate manufacturers. Instead of concentrating on selling to grocery chains, to which it only sells very small amounts, Zotter focuses on delicatessens, confectioneries, wine shops and souvenir shops at airports and museums.

The example of Zotter shows that there is no such thing as a niche that is too small! And that is the secret of the success of clever business

Figure 2.8 Chocolate with Chili Santa Fe – Zotter mixes unusual flavours

Source: Zotter Schokoladen Manufaktur GmbH

unconventionalists. They know what true positioning is, and that it depends on the successful interplay of factors inside and outside the company: on aligning your core competences with the wishes and desires of clearly defined target groups.

Business unconventionalists in super-niches: Karmann & Co

With the first rays of summer sunshine, the convertibles are out on the road and they are in great demand by sunloving drivers. And no one is happier about that than Europe's biggest producer of convertibles, Karmann in Osnabruck, Germany. The company was founded in 1901 and has elegantly positioned itself in the difficult automotive suppliers market. Karmann specializes in the development and construction of convertibles and coupes, concentrating exclusively on business-to-business sales to car makers. It does not sell directly to the consumer.

Few people are aware, for example, that Karmann produces the Mercedes CLK convertible, and that the Audi A4 convertible, the new Beetle convertible and the Chrysler sports coupe Crossfire also come from Osnabruck. Karmann has become the extended workshop for many of the big car makers.

The company sees itself as a contract manufacturer called in by the car producers to help them meet demand when their own production capacity is not sufficient. And it is even happier when car makers have their new models produced exclusively by Karmann. It is cheaper for the automobile manufacturer to do so, as vehicles like convertibles or coupes appeal only to a limited target group and it is expensive to integrate their production into the production of the overall series.

Aircraft seats for the world market

You probably won't have noticed it, even though you may have sat on them at some time: about 55 per cent of all aircraft seats are covered with fabric manufactured by the Swiss company Lantal. The company also supplies around 35 per cent of all floor coverings in aircraft. The special features of the textiles produced by Lantal make them so attractive: Lantal fabrics are self-cleaning and fireproof but at the same time light and elegant. These are central considerations for Lantal's customers, which require fabrics that are not only lightweight, but also easy-care, helping them to cut costs on every single flight.

The world's main airlines all rely on Lantal for their fabrics. To cater more easily to the needs of this clientele, Lantal has established subsidiaries in Seattle and Toulouse – not by coincidence, but because Boeing and Airbus are located there.

Filling an important need with business unconventionality: wheelchair travel

Wolfgang Grabowski created his own market: He organizes trips to India, the Caribbean or the Vatican for people confined to wheelchairs, thus proving that even on the embattled travel market, there is still money to be made with clever ideas. The 43-year-old owner and managing director describes Grabo-Tours as the leading European travel company for special needs groups, with 2,000 regular customers in the German-speaking countries. Each year, Grabo-Tours organizes 50 different tour packages: a quasi-monopoly.

Grabowski also had a personal motive in setting up the company. His brother Peter has been confined to a wheelchair since a serious car accident. When Wolfgang and his brother planned to go on holiday together for the first time since the crash, they soon discovered that the colourful, carefree world of the glossy travel brochures with its clear blue skies, relaxation at the poolside and sightseeing tours did not cater to the needs of people with handicaps.

Grabowski's holidays cost between 10 and 25 per cent more than the package tours offered by other travel companies, but the company offers much more than the standard package tour. On each of the tours, in addition to the tour guide, there are three or four aides available around the clock to help the travellers. (These volunteers are not paid for their services, but they get the holiday free of charge.) And Wolfgang Grabowski emphasizes that a hotel needs at least four stars before he will even consider it.

Grabowski's greatest capital is his network and personal initiative. The network helps him to realize even the craziest ideas. And to ensure that things go smoothly, the boss himself repeatedly tests the locations to make sure that they really do cater to the special needs of his clientele. All this makes him a very busy man, but it enables him to keep his promise: Grabo will make it possible.

Business unconventionalists work up steam – but not hot air

The company sells only one product – and is the world leader. Rational AG in Landsberg am Lech is the unchallenged market leader for steam cooking systems for hotel, restaurant and canteen kitchens. In 1976 it launched its 'Combi-steamer' on the market for professional kitchen technology. At the time, the idea of preparing food gently and quickly using a combination of steam and hot air was revolutionary.

Rational AG recognized the market potential for its new technology, and carved out a new niche for itself in the market for hotel and restaurant kitchens and canteens. For 20 years the company has dominated this market, and in 1997 it took the next leap forward with a new technology: Rational's 'Combi-Plus' was the first device that made it possible to cook food automatically in complex, multi-stage processes. This meant that the equipment could now be operated by less qualified personnel without compromising on the quality.

Above all, this new technology gave Rational a new competitive edge over its competitors. At the same time, it meant that the company was no longer simply a supplier of hardware. The main factors that contributed to the success of the system are the software, the cooking process itself and the user-friendly operation of the equipment. As Rational's target group is clearly defined and the relevant statistics readily available, it was easy to assess market penetration and growth potential. To ensure further expansion, Rational does not rely on its technological edge alone, but employs trained chefs as sales specialists and has established a worldwide service network.

The example of Rational AG shows that the best way to 'own' a market is to create it yourself. Ideally it will be a completely new market that did not exist before and will be defined by the product itself. The product has to remain unique. Continual improvement will be necessary in order to defend its position.

A niche for the bare facts: Naked-Air & Naked News

Imagine that you have switched on your computer to catch up on the latest world news. Suddenly, as she is reporting on the latest bomb attack in Iraq, the female newsreader starts to peel off the jacket of her conservative two-piece suit. As she reads the next news bulletin about an earthquake in Japan, she unbuttons her blouse and reveals a black lacy bra. Slowly, she slides the straps down over her shoulders ...

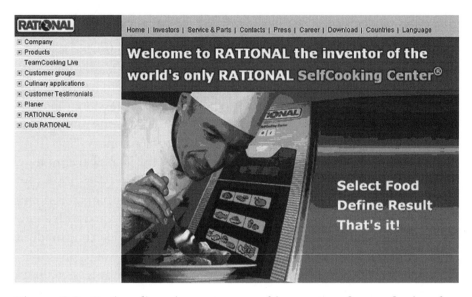

Figure 2.9 Rational's unique steam cooking system for professional chefs

Source: Rational AG, www.rational-ag.de

On the website www.nakednews.com, the news is presented with a difference. It may not be to everyone's liking, but it has an audience of millions. The difference between this show, which is produced in Toronto and was launched in 1999, and the standard evening news lies not in the content but in the female newsreaders, who strip while they read the news.

Naked News is a daily entertainment and news broadcast with a potential weekly audience of some 34 million in the United States and several million in Great Britain, Australia and more than 170 other countries.

Naked News, the naked airlines Naked-Air, a company that offers cruises for nudists: there seem to be no limits to the creativity of businesspeople catering to this format. And though their ideas may seem slightly scandalous and crazy, it has to be admitted that they are smart! They show the importance of a narrow focus. If you try to be all things to all people and offer a wide range of products and services on many different markets and for many different target groups, you will always run the risk of being average at best. On the other hand, if you focus on tailoring a product or service to one specific segment of the market, you can be extremely successful.

Proof of this is the 'Freedom Paradise' in Cancun, Mexico. The idea: People with rather generous proportions don't have an easy time of it. They may come across as jovial, intelligent and clever as television detectives or talk show hosts, but the hard reality of life is a different one, especially on a beach holiday, when they find themselves continually subjected to the curious and critical scrutiny of the slim and athletic people around them. A clever hotel owner saw potential here – and opened the first beach club for corpulent people in Cancun. At Freedom Paradise, all the guests have fuller figures – a simple, but very effective focus. Objectively, the king-sized holiday club hardly differs from the other hotels in Cancun. Its positioning alone makes it unique. It has higher capacity utilization and gets free PR all over the world – even in this book! And yet the idea is as simple as it is ingenious.

Naked airline Naked-Air enjoys a similar position, though the business idea is somewhat more risqué. It is the first airline in the world to offer nudist flights on selected routes – and is successful. Its flights are fully booked weeks in advance. By cornering a clear niche for itself, the company remains unaffected by economic cycles and crises. It doesn't have to worry that established airlines may try to break into its market, and it profits from word-of-mouth advertising within its target group.

Suddenly the idea of offering Mediterranean cruises for nudists doesn't seem all that crazy any more. The first European nudist cruise sailed from Barcelona in 2004 and called at Ibiza, Ajaccio and Nice before returning to Barcelona. It's certainly not the largest target group in the world, but guess how many people signed up for this first nudist cruise: 50? 100? 250? The answer is 450 people from 17 countries! The oldest passenger was 74, the youngest just two weeks old.

Again, you can see that these companies created their own markets, not in competition with the established providers but by cleverly cornering a niche the big companies had no interest in.

Business unconventionality box

We defined personality as a market niche. We seek to amaze, surprise, entertain.

> Herb Kelleher, former Chairman and CEO, Southwest Airlines

Be bold and discover a niche or create one for yourself! In order to do so, first answer this important question:

What is our Unique Selling Proposition (USP)?

- What does our company stand for?
- What do we do better than the rest?
- What do we have that excites our customers and our employees?

Why ask what excites your employees? Because long-term success is only possible when every member of your team has understood where the company's strengths lie. Companies – like individuals – need their own identity in order to stand out from the mass. And only when your employees live that corporate identity will your customers too get the message.

Remember Josef Zotter from Styria in Austria and his hand-scooped chocolate, and Grabowski-Tours, which specializes in arranging travel for the handicapped and the able-bodied. The moral of the story: there's no such thing as a niche that is too small.

---

3 Different thinking: products

'We understand our customers' needs and make every effort to satisfy them.' Twenty years ago, this slogan would have had real value for customers. Nowadays, it's just not going to turn any heads. Companies that do no more than satisfy their customers' requirements will be lucky to hold their own. Customers today are more demanding, more aggressive, more impatient and astute than ever before, and – what's even worse – they have a bigger range of products and services than ever before to choose from.

It's no longer about companies selling things. Today it is customers who decide what they want to buy. At first glance it might seem that this is splitting hairs, but in fact it is an accurate description of the great challenge faced by companies today. Products and services have to please the consumer, and companies have to get customers to choose their products above all others – for whatever reasons!

In the first two chapters, we looked at innovative business strategies and new markets. Now we shall turn our attention to the core of our business activities: the products and services we offer to the customer.

The title of the chapter is simply 'Products', although in fact this covers a complex framework of material and immaterial characteristics of the goods we offer our customers, ranging from functionality and design to additional services and, last but not least, the emotional factors determined by advertising and the influence of the 'community'.

So this chapter is of relevance for you even if you are in the service sector. The borders between actual products and services are becoming more and more blurred. It is hardly possible to offer a product today without additional services. In fact, the decisive factors on which customers make their decision to buy are often the services offered and market positioning. Our examples can show you as a service provider how to offer more innovative services. Even design considerations can be of decisive importance in the services sector – so read on and find out more!

To be truly innovative, you need to be daring and unconventional. In other words, you need to practise business unconventionality. And if you have set yourself the goal of introducing new and unconventional products and services, you are not going to find the new ideas you need simply by studying the competition and poring over the specialist publications for your industry. The ideas you may find there will at best make your company and your products a close imitation of all the others on your market, but they won't make you a business unconventionalist. To be a business unconventionalist and enter the market with cool and innovative products, you need the ability to differentiate yourself from the rest of the field and to continually redefine your company and your products. But in order to be different, you first have to think differently. And that's why this book is as much about the way you think as the way you act in business life.

Product DNA: question existing product concepts

No matter what industry you're in, you will have no difficulty explaining exactly why your product is the way it is and presumably why it couldn't be any other way. We have a whole array of preconceptions, views and 'unshakeable' principles regarding our industry, what our competition is and who our customers are. And of course, we also think we know precisely which products our customers want and which they don't want.

> Most people in an industry are blind in the same way. They're all paying attention to the same things, and NOT paying attention to the same things.
>
> Gary Hamel, strategy guru

And these preconceived ideas we have are constantly reinforced and confirmed by information we receive from colleagues, competitors, through the press and at conferences we attend. Such events are always attended by the same old representatives of the industry; we read the same books and magazines and are of course always ready to copy from our competitors any idea that is even vaguely new. This fund of 'inside knowledge' determines the range and predictability of management action. It forms a framework and imposes boundaries for innovative thinking within a company. It defines which ideas are considered 'acceptable', and which are off the mark.

As a result, we come to look at the world through the perspective of our own industry, and our acceptance of these seemingly irrefutable conventions of the industry and all the preconceptions and opinions that go with it become an intellectual straitjacket. This in turn makes companies perceive only part of the picture and not the whole picture.

The trick – and it is much more difficult than it sounds for companies caught within such a rigid conventional mindset – is to cast away the mental restraints of this product concept and ask yourself, 'Why is it like that?', 'Does it really have to be like that?' and 'Have we in fact got the whole picture or just parts of it?'

> Paradoxically, the ability to forget the old answers, to unlearn the old ways, becomes a decisive factor for success in a business environment which is changing at the speed of light.
>
> Jonas Ridderstråle, co-author of the book *Funky Business*

Rule 8 of business unconventionality

Product DNA: question existing product concepts.

Conventional thinking: you accept existing product concepts and strive to optimize your range of products and services within these limits.
Business unconventionality: you question established product concepts and gain new scope for innovative and cool products and services.

Take James Dyson as an example. He is the man who reinvented the vacuum cleaner. If Dyson had simply accepted preconceived ideas, beliefs and seemingly 'unshakeable' conceptions of what a vacuum cleaner should look like and how it should work, he would probably never have tackled this monumental task. He would probably simply have thought, like all the other manufacturers of vacuum cleaners, 'If it were possible to make a better vacuum cleaner, Miele, Siemens and Electrolux would have done it long ago.' But Dyson ignored the established concepts: his approach was more that of the 'crazy genius'.

It isn't necessarily good just because it's an established concept

The fact that no one had ever set out to reinvent the vacuum cleaner didn't deter Dyson. In fact, he took it as an open invitation. And there is one other important thing about James Dyson: he is a restless spirit who hates nothing more than the status quo. His own personal dissatisfaction with conventional solutions led him to reinvent the vacuum cleaner. Dyson found it unacceptable for consumers that the suction power of conventional vacuum cleaners drops off sharply shortly after you have put in a new dust bag. In other words, for years the industry had been selling products that didn't function effectively.

You may be thinking, well, if that's all he had to worry about! But if that had been the only problem in his life, James Dyson would have been a happy man. A closer look at Dyson's background, however, reveals that in 1978, the year in which he decided to do something about the problem of badly functioning vacuum cleaners, Dyson was working full-time on the design and development of gardening equipment, not a very profitable sector at the time, so he had more than enough other worries on his mind. But Dyson is an unconventionalist who likes to get to the bottom of things. Once he had discovered that changing the dust bag on the vacuum cleaner only improved the suction power for a short time, he cut the bag open to find out why. It didn't take him long to find the cause of the problem: the bag has fine pores intended to keep the dust in while allowing the sucked-in air to circulate. The problem was that the dust clogs the pores so that the air can no longer circulate freely. And if the airflow is restricted, the suction power of the vacuum cleaner decreases sharply.

What does this teach us? Just because the manufacturers of vacuum cleaners have been selling cleaners equipped with dust bags for more

Figure 3.1 Dyson vacuum cleaners – high suction cleaning
Source: Dyson GmbH

than a century, it doesn't necessarily mean that this was the right approach. In the very apt words of Kurt Tucholsky, 'Never trust an expert who tells you he's been doing things that way for 20 years. It could be he's been doing it wrong for 20 years!'

The VIP model vacuum cleaner

Dyson was motivated to develop a vacuum cleaner that functions far better than all the rest – and without a dust bag. He replaced the traditional bag with two cyclone chambers that cannot become clogged up.

The outer cyclone spins out larger dust and dirt particles, while the inner cyclone accelerates the airflow in order to remove even the smallest particles. This unique new technology quickly made Dyson's vacuum cleaner market leader in Great Britain, and – this is the good news for Mr Dyson – he makes a turnover of millions with his innovative products. His customers include such famous names as Sarah Jessica Parker, Sharon Osbourne, Elton John, Kylie Minogue, Tony Blair and the Queen – although we have it on authority that the last two in the list are hardly likely to be pushing the cleaner around themselves.

If you imagine that James Dyson has now retired to his house on the Bermudas in order to enjoy a carefree life spending his millions, you would be wrong. He is and always has been a restless spirit. When someone said to him, 'I love your vacuum cleaner, but when are you going to make one you don't have to push around?' he set out to develop the Dyson DC06 robot vacuum cleaner, which cleans not only thoroughly, but automatically and more systematically than a human being would. And since pushing the cleaner around occasionally is not our only household chore, Dyson was ready with another new invention: the Dyson washing machine. Replicating the movements we perform when washing laundry by hand, the Dyson engineers constructed an innovative washing machine with two drums rotating simultaneously in opposite directions. The Dyson Contrarotator was launched on the British market in 2002: the first washing machine with two contra-rotating drums. As the Contrarotator removes dirt more effectively, it washes faster, has a greater load capacity and washes much cleaner than traditional washing machines.

What is Dyson's next project? We don't know, but we are sure he already has his eye on the next household device, and is already investigating new approaches in accordance with the following rules:

> Don't just accept it when people say, 'This is the only way to do it' and 'We've always done it that way.' Phrases like that should just fire your imagination.

> If you're dissatisfied with the conventional solution, change it!

Surprising innovations: reinventing the smallest room

We have seen that it is possible to question a product concept and then in the next step, reinvent it. It has worked with vacuum cleaners and washing machines. But can you reinvent the toilet? Toilets are mainly standardized products serving just one purpose. Innovations are rare here. In fact, it was a minor sensation when some restaurants installed toilets with self-cleaning seats.

You only have to visit Japan to see that it *is* possible to reinvent the toilet. The Japanese love toilets, and in particular, luxury toilets. They are so obsessed with toilets that you can even buy special street maps with names like 'Tokyo's paradise for your posterior', which show you which hotels, shops and restaurants offer the best toilets.

For foreign visitors to Japan, it takes some getting used to. When you enter a bathroom, you receive a friendly greeting and are confronted with an instrument panel that looks like something taken from the cockpit of a Boeing 747. But Japan's high-tech loos represent a huge innovation. While most other manufacturers limit themselves to such half-hearted changes as a new design or offering the toilet in beige, light blue or mint green instead of only in white, Toto and Intax, Japan's biggest producers of toilets, are racing each other to launch the next innovations. Together, they hold over 90 per cent of the market, and the winning features of their products include seats with adjustable heating, toilets that neutralize odours automatically by means of air purifiers and filters and actually give the visitor's bottom a shower – which can be adjusted to the desired strength and temperature. And if that's not enough to make you happy, there are also toilets that can carry out body fat or urine analyses. Toto has just developed a model for diabetics that measures blood sugar levels. There are long-term plans to incorporate a whole battery of medical tests into Toto toilets. Data protectionists are even warning that the police could install toilets that carry out automatic drug tests in public buildings. What a potential market for Toto!

The definition of a lousy product? Everyone in the company loves it

This example shows that even the most profane of products can be reinvented and turned into something consumers will be happy to dig deeper into their pockets for: Toto toilets cost up to US$3,000, and particularly sophisticated models even more. If the Japanese can manage to turn such a mundane product into a cult object and sell it for a corresponding price, what excuse have you got for not trying it with your product?

Think revolution, not evolution.

Richard Sullivan, Home Depot

No matter how commonplace your products or services are, your company must be filled with the spirit of continual innovation. The questions 'Why is it like that?' and 'Does it really have to be like that?' should be familiar questions in your everyday business life. But you won't get your staff to internalize this basic attitude to innovation simply by calling for 'more unconventional thinking'. The willingness to continually question the status quo and to look over the rim of your teacup every single day is not something you can simply order in a

Figure 3.2 Get your health check-up in the smallest room – Toto toilets do more!

Source: Toto USA Inc, www.totousa.com

management directive: 'With immediate effect, all members of staff will now become business unconventionalists.'

Business unconventionality means encouraging people to experiment. But the big disadvantage of experiments is that they are risky! They might be successful, but then again, they might not. A company that wants to encourage business unconventionality has to have a high error tolerance level. Failure could even be said to be the foundation for success.

> The fastest way to succeed is to double your failure rate.
>
> Thomas Watson senior, founder and former CEO of IBM

The problem is that many companies don't really offer an environment that openly embraces mistakes. There is hardly any tolerance for making all the stupid mistakes in the beginning and for making them fast in order to succeed sooner. On the contrary, in many companies, making a mistake means that you can look forward to spending the rest of your time in the firm's own version of the Corporate Siberia. The message is loud and clear: mistakes will be punished. This doesn't stop employees from making mistakes, but it certainly prevents them trying out anything new in the future. It is the surest way to develop a corporate culture where innovation and business unconventionality are neatly nipped in the bud.

Errors and failures are pointers to change and innovation and must not be penalized. They are the only way to learn not to make the same mistake twice. Jack Welch, the charismatic former CEO of General Electric, once said, 'I rewarded mistakes by giving people bonuses for making them, because they kept the company on its toes.' That doesn't mean that it's a cushy job working at GE and that you can afford to slack off now and then. On the contrary, Welch ruled with an iron hand, but he had a good intuition for the soft skills. He devoted most of his energy and the greater part of his working day to dealing with the human side of business. 'We select our staff and pay them. No one is told how they are to go about their everyday business.' The freedom to try something new and the ability to learn quickly from mistakes remain important criteria in the management style of GE.

GE and other successful and innovative firms show that our businesses need to become breeding grounds for people willing to take risks. And in order to achieve this, they must have a high tolerance level for errors, because it is a simple fact that we learn more from our mistakes than from our successes.

You must not be deterred by the notorious prophets of doom and pessimists. We all know that for every innovation, there are hundreds of so-called experts who warn against it. When the printing press was invented, monks complained that the new books were much more anonymous than their own handwritten manuscripts. Sceptics warned that railway travel could be bad for the health and that the telephone would isolate people, as they would no longer need to leave their homes. If we had listened to all these professional sceptics, we would probably still be sitting around in dark caves.

Don't get us wrong here: we are not saying that you should totally ignore criticism. We would simply like to point out that you should register the criticism, but take it with a healthy dose of scepticism. Or, to put it another way, you should be very, very sceptical if you present your new idea and your toughest critics are over the moon about it. This is a phenomenon described by Arno Penzias, a Nobel prize-winner from Bell Labs: 'The definition of a lousy product is, everyone in the company loves it.'

Adding new functions to a product: the Oral-B factor

Established product concepts need to be continually questioned, and the search for the new and the different should become second nature. One way of challenging the established product concept is to add a new function. The toothbrush is a good example. In the last 20 years, the classic model 'handle with brush' has been not only improved but also expanded to include many other functions. The result: today, you can spend well over €200 on a dental centre with ultrasound cleaning and water pick function.

That wasn't always so. In the 1970s, the electric toothbrush was considered the most useless product ever developed. But in the late 1980s Peter Hilfinger, now head of research at Braun Oral-B, had an idea that was so good that the Braun factory in Marktheidenfeld in Germany has long since produced its five millionth battery-operated toothbrush.

Hilfinger, who originally developed electric shavers, asked himself why sales of electric toothbrushes had been so sluggish, and that for 20 years. He recognized that the conventional models did nothing more than imitate the movement of the human hand, with a rectangular brush head that simply moved to and fro. 'And all at once,' he says 'all at once it hit me: it needed a round head. A head that moved in a way no human hand can move!' It was that simple. The innovative feature was the circular movement of the brush head. Later this was replaced by a rapid oscillating movement. And sales were also helped along by the fact that dentists recommended the product to their patients.

Customers don't buy products, they buy results

Today, more than 30 per cent of German households own an electric toothbrush. More than half of them are Braun-Oral-B toothbrushes, a brand that belongs to US corporation Gillette. In the stagnating oral hygiene sector, Braun Oral-B notched up sales of more than €1 billion in Germany alone in the year 2003, with two-digit growth-rates for electric toothbrushes; over 50 per cent growth in numbers, and 69 per cent in value.

The next product generation is already in the stores: the sonic toothbrush as the latest weapon against plaque. According to the makers, the ultrasonic waves work without the brush even touching the teeth. Even top scientists rave about the quality of the sonic toothbrushes and see them as a milestone in the history of dental hygiene. The customer is hardly in a position to judge the truth of that statement and has to accept the claims of the manufacturers. The ads promise three-stage cleaning for teeth, gums and tongue, a high-frequency cleaning system and above all, a new concept for comprehensive dental care. Who could say no to that?

Question the price–performance ratio: cheap operations

Another way to challenge existing product concepts is to question established ideas about the price–performance ratio – and revolutionize them. The Berlin Klinik für Minimal Invasive Chirurgie (MIC) (clinic for minimal invasive surgery) shows how this can be done. Patients who are insured under the state health system, over 80 per cent of MIC's patients, receive four-star treatment – and not just in the operating theatre.

This example is all the more remarkable in that it originated in Germany and not in the United States or Singapore. And it comes from an industry which is the subject of more discussion than any other, proving that things can be done differently, even in hospital care and the healthcare system.

Shorter hospital stays, inexpensive but profitable surgical procedures, satisfied customers: impossible in Germany, if you believe the discussion about health reforms. Yet MIC patients with state health insurance receive four-star treatment: their baggage is taken to their rooms, they can take their meals in a bistro, there is a lounge where they can listen to music and a patio where they can enjoy the sunshine, and all these are standard services in this 34-bed clinic. Patients can also enjoy a morning lie-in, receive personal care and even listen to their favourite CD in the operating theatre.

It all sounds too good to be true – or at least like a prime loss maker, but this specialized surgical clinic has made a profit ever since it opened in November 1997. The 'trick' is the use of cutting-edge technology which in turn means that patients are ready to go home faster, thereby reducing costs enormously. Patients check in at the clinic just three hours before their operation and are allowed home as soon as possible. The average hospital stay at MIC is 1.7 days. In addition, personnel costs at the clinic, which is run as a private limited company, are 30 per cent lower than at comparable state-run hospitals. Doctors and other medical staff are only required to administer medical treatment, while a ward secretary takes care of administrative tasks and meals are served by hotel-trained personnel. By comparison, in state-run hospitals, highly paid doctors spend up to 40 per cent of their time on administrative tasks.

This example demonstrates that it is possible not only to question the entire product concept even in a very inflexible, difficult industry, but also to successfully innovate there.

Naïve-innovative: be like children

Children are naïve. They know nothing of what is possible and what is impossible, and so they ask questions like 'Why is the sky blue?', 'Why is water wet?', 'Why can't you see the air?' and 'Why are you my parents?' Grown-ups, on the other hand, are clever. They know what is possible and what isn't.

So adults fob the children off with answers like 'That's just the way it is.' Yet it is this naïve approach, this continual asking 'Why?', 'How?' and 'What?' that is the mark of the business unconventionalist. Does

Figure 3.3 For the pampered palate – the Ikarus restaurant in Hangar 7 at Salzburg airport
Source: Red Bull Hangar-7 GmbH & CoKG, UlrichGrill.com

that make business unconventionalists naïve? No. They have simply retained a certain childlike sense of curiosity and the ability to question things without preconceived ideas.

Eckart Witzigmann, for example, the 'Chef of the Century', has kept his unbiased perspective on things. For him, the answer to the question 'Why does the same chef cook every night in a restaurant?' wasn't 'Because that's just the way it is.' Instead, the question laid the foundation for an innovative gastronomy concept: the Ikarus restaurant in Hangar 7 of Salzburg airport. The innovative feature: every month, a new top chef cooks there. The schedule for the year can be found at www.hangar-7.com.

Asking questions gets you places: hearing aids and loans

British pharmaceutical retailer Boots also found an interesting answer to an unbiased question: why do the batteries in hearing aids need to be replaced? The answer: there's no need. In Great Britain, you can now buy disposable hearing aids from Boots. It's not an environmentally friendly solution, perhaps, but for some customers it is a blessing, because up to now they had to have new batteries fitted by a specialist.

As a result they didn't get them replaced often enough and at times didn't hear very well because the batteries were getting weak.

In the United States, clever business executives have come up with a completely new business idea based on the seemingly paradoxical question, why isn't it possible to combine the advantages of digital photography – being able to view the pictures and select the ones you want before printing them out – with the principle of the cheap disposable camera? The answer: the first disposable digital cameras are now on the market. Once the memory is full, you send in the whole camera. The cost of the photos is included in the price, and the cameras themselves are recycled.

And another example of an unbiased question, this time from the banking sector: why do you have to wait days or even weeks to hear whether you can have a loan? Norisbank found the answer: private loans can be approved in just 30 seconds, by computer via the internet. The computer decides whether the loan is granted, an automatic scoring system takes care of risk control. This easyCredit, as the bank called its product, is a huge success and has drastically reduced consumers' misgivings about approaching a bank for a loan.

All these examples show that very mundane products and established business concepts offer extraordinary scope for new ideas if you are only creative enough. It is possible to completely reinvent not only tangible products but also services and processes. Naïve, unbiased questions are the key to the door leading us to entirely new product concepts, because these are the questions that will force us to come up with a smart answer.

Business unconventionality box

You see things and you say: Why? But I dream things that never were, and I say: Why not?

> George Bernard Shaw, Irish writer and Nobel Prize winner

No matter how commonplace your company's products or services may be, they must be embedded in a culture of continuous innovation. The questions 'Why is that so?' and 'Does it have to be like that?' must become the everyday tools of your business life. Question established product concepts and gain new scope for innovative and cool products and services!

Remember James Dyson, the man who reinvented the vacuum cleaner, and toilet producers Toto, who revolutionized the image of 'the smallest room'. Business unconventionalists can be found on all markets and in all industries. They successfully challenge conventional product concepts and fly in the face of the seemingly irrefutable rules of our business sectors.

Design matters: design as a competitive factor

'The man is out of his mind!', 'Fire him on the spot!' 'Stop Chris Bangle! Don't let him ruin any more of your beautiful BMWs!' In these and other similar protests, motorists from all over the world called on BMW to fire chief designer Chris Bangle. The reason for all the fuss? Bangle had restyled BMW's flagship Series 7 sedan with sculpted curves and contours. The car's bulbous trunk was ridiculed as the 'Bangle butt', and thousands signed an internet petition imploring BMW to 'Stop Chris Bangle'.

Some saw Bangle as 'the Devil's Draughtsman' – others as a design god. One thing is clear from the example of BMW. Design polarizes, and it is definitely one way to get people talking about your products again, in this case the new Series 7. For despite the fact that in the first flush of feeling, some BMW enthusiasts were quite extreme in their views – 'Buy him a ticket to India, so he can go and work for Tata (an Indian car manufacturer). They've got no design to ruin!' – one thing is now clear: the new design boosted sales for the Munich car maker.

Business unconventionalists realize that design is far more than just a step in the process with the sole purpose of embellishing products. Companies like hi-fi manufacturer Bang & Olufsen, whose competitive edge rests to a large extent on the design of its products, or car makers Audi, VW, BMW, Porsche and Mercedes Benz are all living proof of the power and significance of design. Or take Braun, some of whose products are now on display at New York's Museum of Modern Art. Innovative Braun design has been the hallmark of the product range since 1955, and is the foundation for the success and the image of the company. Or office chair producers Vitra and Wilkhahn, or boiler manufacturers Viessmann and Buderus – they all show that design can be the backbone of overall corporate strategy and the most crucial factor for the success of a product or service. Design triggers passion, emotion, affinity, and can therefore form the basis for emotional differentiation.

Rule 9 of business unconventionality

Design matters: design as a competitive factor.

Conventional thinking: you focus on your products and their function – design is the least important step and serves solely to make products more aesthetically pleasing.

Business unconventionality: you take advantage of unusual design to differentiate your products and make them successful. The design of products, packaging and sales outlets will thus become an integral component of your corporate strategy!

Design sells

Sony knows! Former president and CEO Norio Ohga says, 'At Sony, we assume that all products of our competitors have basically the same technology, price, performance and features. Design is the only thing that differentiates one product from another in the marketplace.'

Kartell knows! Its hard plastic furniture with its superior design has become a best-seller, enabling the company to achieve positive growth rates in a sliding market. Kartell embodies the latest trends, aided by top designers like Philippe Starck.

The car makers know – and are rediscovering the factor design. After years of monotony, years in which all the cars we saw on the streets had the same practical but unimaginative design, the big groups are now opting for more extravagant forms – not least because of the keen competition. 'There are no really bad cars today,' says Othmar Wickenheiser, head of the International Design Centre in Berlin. 'That's why design is becoming a crucial differentiating factor more and more.' And the car makers are putting this maxim into practice: Renault, for example, woos consumers with models with very unusual design and which thus stand out very clearly from the rest of the field.

Design wins hearts

At Renault, there was little opposition from within the company to the introduction of these striking designs – perhaps because Renault's chief designer Patrick le Quément is the only designer worldwide with a seat and a vote on the board of directors. Of course, many other companies have now also recognized that design is a decisive competitive factor. Chrysler, for example, after making million-dollar losses, now plans to solve its problems by launching products with 'exciting design'. Bob Lutz, the driving force behind the upswing at Chrysler in the early 1990s and a legend in the world of US car making, has gone back to work for former rivals General Motors at the age of 69, and promises customers 'Cars to fall in love with'. Even conservative German car maker Opel with its staid, rather boring image, advertises 'fresh thinking' and has given the medium-range Vectra and compact car Astra some striking and extremely sleek lines (by the standards of Opel models).

© Christian HOUDEK für RENAUl

Figure 3.4 Renault – striking the balance between mass production and avant garde

Source: Renault Nissan Austria

Consumers may love or hate your latest model, but there's one thing you have to prevent at all costs: they must never be indifferent to it. 'Nowadays it's not enough to appeal to the customers' intellect,' says Opel's chief designer, Hans Seer. 'We have to win their hearts.' And all manufacturers are following more or less the same strategy. Design is not only a question of giving a product a more attractive appearance. It is increasingly becoming a means to gain that competitive edge and differentiate yourself clearly from the rest of the field.

'For years, we were looking for our own formal language to give our top-range models an identity all their own,' said Renault's chief designer Le Quément in an interview with the German business magazine *Wirtschaftswoche*. And it desperately needed an identity: for years, Renault had more or less restricted itself to copying the luxury models of BMW and Mercedes, and had to be content with the crumbs that fell from the table. 'Of course we are taking a risk,' Le Quément freely admits, 'but it would be even more of a risk not to risk anything at all.'

Design as a work of art

Good design is achieved by following certain basic principles in the pursuit of clearly defined goals. But there is another aspect that has to be taken into consideration: it doesn't always have to be the product itself that receives an innovative new design. There are three basic areas for design innovation:

- **Product design**: here, the focus of the design process really is on the product itself. Of course, the form of the product often plays a decisive role in generating an emotional or functional tie. But what if you sell petrol? Are you going to dye it green to make it seem more environmentally friendly – or red and gold to symbolize how powerful it will make your engine? Here, your possibilities and the effect that can be achieved are limited.
- **Packaging design**: here, we mean packaging in the broadest sense. The design of packaging can have a tremendous effect, and you can even deliberately go for the 'non-designed' look, for example to emphasize low-price products.
- **Sales outlet design**: the shopping experience itself is becoming increasingly important. Many companies are opening flagship stores to ensure a cohesive brand presence. Nothing is left to chance in the design of banks, supermarkets, coffee shops or fast food restaurants.

Often you will find that the products of innovative, successful companies are in a way a sort of overall work of art. Product, packaging and sales outlet are all carefully coordinated for maximum effect. In the following examples, note how symbioses are formed here.

By the way, no matter whether you are a producer of industrial goods (B2B) or consumer goods (B2C), it is always important to be conscious of design as a competitive factor. Don't let anyone tell you differently. There is always a close link between design and brand, the properties associated with a product, how easily it will be identified and recognized by consumers. These are factors that are just as important in the industrial goods sector as in the consumer goods market.

Design symbiosis with cult status: furniture by Kartell

'Today, design is the most important factor, even more important than functionality and price,' says Japanese architect Kiyoshi Sakashita. Big names such as Braun, Alessi and Bang & Olufsen, whose products have

Figure 3.5 Bang & Olufsen – hi-fi, television or art?
Source: Bang & Olufsen Germany

achieved cult status with their buyers, confirm this statement. But how do you attain such cult status by means of design? Let's take a closer look at the products of Italian furniture manufacturer Kartell. Its range includes chairs, sofas, tables, drawer systems, bookshelves, and also accessories like umbrella stands and magazine racks. And the special feature? The entire range is made out of plastic, a material that can be used anywhere, is stable, durable and easy to process.

Design is a central element of Kartell's strategy, and one which allows the company to differentiate itself clearly. The company draws inspiration for its innovative shapes, colours and finishings from vehicle construction, the beverage industry and many other sectors. But Kartell goes even further than that; product design, corporate design and store design must enter into a symbiosis in which the two most important roles are played by the designer and the interior designer.

Kartell works with well-known international designers like Ron Arad and Philippe Starck. The aim is that each of its core products should reflect both the spirit of the company and the spirit of the designer. Each designer has his or her own distinctive hallmark. Ron Arad has a penchant for curvy lines, as his 'Bookworm' bookshelves show. Antonio Citterio focuses on a broad functionality, Piero Lissoni on geometry.

This Italian furniture producer came close to bankruptcy in 1976, but has since staged an amazing comeback by using design to create a unique position for itself on the market. Kartell's products combine quality and trendy design with a sensible price–performance ratio.

Develop emotional design: Apple forever

Business unconventionalists know that on the markets of the future, only companies whose products have a clear profile and are perceived as superior by the consumer will be successful. In the struggle for differentiation, identification and customer loyalty, design is becoming a central success factor.

> Fifteen years ago, companies competed on price, today it's quality, tomorrow it's design.
>
> Robert Hayes, Professor at the Harvard Business School

And another thing is clear: products that are to survive as brand names will no longer be able to do so simply by virtue of their function. Instead, they must be seen as aids to fulfilling individual and emotional requirements.

Computer manufacturer Apple also realized that its customers weren't buying its products simply because they performed well. Along with innovative products, design is the decisive success factor. Take the iMac as an example. Apple's idea was to develop an internet PC that was inexpensive, easy to operate and at the same time pleasing to look at. Until then, computers had only been available with housing in mousy grey or plaque-yellow. Apple had the wonderful idea of simply painting its computers in attractive pastel colours. A revolution: no one in the sector had dared to do anything like it before. After the amazing success of the new iMac, which came on the market in August 1998, the new design concept was applied to all new products – and it worked.

Again and again, Apple has set new design trends for the entire industry. The Apple design team has repeatedly won the prestigious Red Dot Award for industrial design, and become Design Team of the Year. In this way, Apple differentiates itself very clearly from its competitors in the PC market, which are still doggedly ignoring the consumer's design preferences. Apple takes a different approach, and the new iMac G5, where the entire computer is integrated in a flat screen, is once again a trendsetter, combining superior performance and beauty.

And of course, Apple has long since expanded its product range to include more than just attractively designed desktop computers. It also makes the very popular MP3 player iPod and the notebook series iBook and PowerBook. High product quality and exclusive design: these are the factors that make Apple very different from other computer manufacturers, and show how product design has made the company a lifestyle manufacturer. Macs are still cult objects: iMac, Cube, iBook or PowerBook, they all look cool and give their owners a certain status. Apple's design department in Cupertino was responsible for the success, and it was hard earned: the team around Jonathan Ive spent three years working on the new concept.

People buy design: Alessi & Co

The Alessi company realized some time ago that the success of a product no longer depends on functionality, technical perfection or quality alone. The Italian company identified appearance, shape and design of its products as decisive factors influencing the customers' decision to buy. Whether it is filigree, airy shapes, futuristic design or cool elegance, Alessi products are works of art that have little in common with Grandma's coffee service or Mum's citrus press.

Designers like Ettore Sottsass, Richard Sapper, Achille Castiglioni, Alessandro Mendini, Aldo Rossi, Michael Graves and Philippe Starck work for the company. Everyday utensils like Sapper's melodic kettle, Sottsass's cruet set, Rossi's espresso machines and Starck's spider-legged citrus press are works of art and icons in the world of consumer goods.

The traditional market for kitchen utensils is stagnating, particularly in Germany, but Alessi has found a solution and now successfully manufactures a wide range of accessories for other areas of the house.

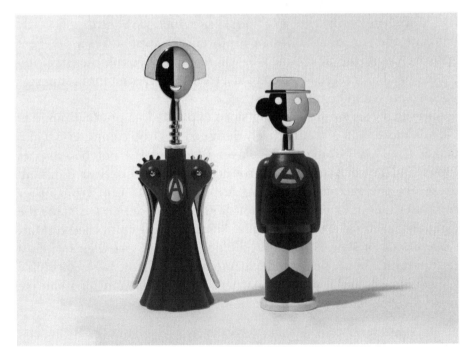

Figure 3.6 Designed for success – the Alessi range
Source: Alessi Showroom, Hamburg

The family-owned company from Italy, founded in 1921, now offers everything from shampoo bottles to complete furniture ranges.

The next market Alessi targeted was the living room. Here too, Alessi is successfully selling its range of designer objects for prices four or five times those of non-designer goods. In partnership with Siemens, Alessi developed a telephone. The Munich electronics giant supplies the technology, while the 'shell' is by the Italian designer team. And Alessi has by no means run out of ideas yet! The company has carved out a niche for itself with product design, and is constantly discovering new fields of activity, for example the Fiat Panda Alessi with its unusual black-and-white bodywork and lime green seat covers.

Design in business-to-business: robots by Kuka

Just take a look around you: in most capital goods sectors, technological progress has led to the creation of a multitude of products of equally high quality. Differentiation by gaining a technological edge would only seem to be possible – if at all – by investing vast sums in research and development. Design, however, offers a clever means of differentiation, particularly in the capital goods industry. Business unconventionalists have long realized this. Design is a means to get ahead, and not only in the consumer goods sector.

Furthermore, on many levels, technological competence only gives you a unique and clear profile in combination with the qualitative aspect of design, while at the same time design provides a promising opportunity to stand out from the rest and escape the anonymity of the conventional product landscape.

With this in mind, the Augsburg-based company Kuka, manufacturer of industrial robots, applied itself to the task of giving its products a more attractive design. The result: while all other robots on the market have angular, functional housing, Kuka designed its robots with organic curves. In addition, Kuka robots were painted in colourful shades, and the company ensured that its logo was not only to be found on the rating plate but was visible from quite a distance on the arm of the robot. And so it is hardly surprising that the Kuka robots won a prestigious design award, the often-mentioned Red Dot Award.

Figure 3.7 Kuka's robots combine technological excellence with unique design

Source: KUKA Roboter GmbH, www.kuka-roboter.de

Packaging as an image-booster: washing-up liquid as a luxury commodity

As the outer casing for the brand, the packaging plays a decisive role in the design and perception of products. With the help of clever packaging, leading brands have been able to successfully establish a clear profile at the point of sale. The cosmetics industry has made this one of its priorities. Packaging design is of crucial importance for perfumes, eau de toilette and other cosmetics. Top designers are hired to create the bottles, and the outer packaging is carefully tailored to fit the image of the product. The days when all cosmetics packaging was made of either glass or cardboard are long gone: companies now use unconventional materials as a means of further differentiating their products, and the figures show that the method works. The more unconventional and emotionally appealing the packaging, the greater the demand for the product!

A few smart young businesspeople observed this phenomenon closely – and asked themselves whether the method only worked for luxury articles. In the true spirit of business unconventionality, they decided to try it out, took a trip to their local supermarket and looked for a run-of-the-mill product whose design they could try to jazz up. They found it amongst the cleaning agents – and their company, Method, proves that packaging design can also be used as a tool to differentiate and boost the image of mundane products like household detergents.

Today, the company has an annual turnover of US$10 million, and rivals giants like Procter & Gamble. The household detergents it sells have basically the same ingredients as the products of its competitors. The only difference is that the bottle was created by a top designer. The challenge: to develop packaging so aesthetically pleasing that customers would be proud to leave it standing on the sink when guests arrive, instead of hiding it in the cupboard.

The household detergents in the Lifestyle range are scented, for example smelling of mint, cucumber, mandarin or lavender, and they are in the premium price range, selling for US$3–5 a bottle. The demand is overwhelming. Method doesn't even produce the detergents itself, but simply puts common or garden detergents into its designer packaging, thus reducing its own risk.

Figure 3.8 Sexy washing-up liquid – how new packaging can turn a household cleaner into a lifestyle product

Source: Method Products Inc, www.methodhome.com

Dreaming up new forms of packaging: sexy gherkins

The market for pickled preserves is stagnating: pickled red cabbage, sauerkraut and gherkins are just not sexy. Traditionally, these are products with an old-fashioned, stuffy image, which are not typically bought by young consumers.

But in accordance with the motto 'Every problem is a hidden opportunity', the Spreewaldhof company, formerly VEB Spreewaldkonserve, took up the challenge and looked at ways to bring fresh impetus to this market. The company is based in Golssen, in the Spree forest south of Berlin. When German consumers hear the word Spreewald, they think of pickled gherkins, and when they hear pickled gherkins they think of Spreewald. It's as simple as that.

What did Spreewald do to update its fuddy-duddy image? It came up with an idea for a very unconventional packaging for its gherkins and achieved a very ambitious goal: it found a way to sell a very uncool product for a high price. The solution: it put large gherkins individually in little tins and sold them as healthy snacks. Get One, a tin containing one large hand-picked gherkin, is sold in petrol stations, supermarkets, discotheques and sports studios as a trendy article for between €1.50–2.50 – quite a sum for one pickled gherkin!

The recipe for success here is that the packaging is not standard for the product, and that is the precise reason why it sells so well. However, the most innovative product in the world won't sell unless people know it's out there. Spreewaldhof found a solution to this problem, too – with the help of a movie. After the box-office success of *Goodbye Lenin!*, everyone knew that Spreewald gherkins were found on every table in East Germany. In the film, the product is cleverly presented and woven into the plot. Advertising partners of the film company? Spreewaldhof! And as a clever spin-off idea, it marketed a gift pack containing a DVD of the film and a single, very fat Spreewald gherkin in a tin: Get One!

Sales outlet design: high-tech at Prada

An important but surprisingly much neglected opportunity for differentiation is the design of sales outlets. Here, it is a matter not only of creating a unique experience – more about that in the next chapter – but of establishing cohesive and future-oriented fields of perception at the point of sale. Successful store concepts like that of Prada or Nike (Niketown) show just how far this idea can be taken.

Italian fashion label Prada employs the very best architects. Star architect Rem Koolhaas created the flagship store in New York, and together with Herzog & de Meuron, Prada has established a further unusual flagship store in Tokyo. Both stores attract attention with their unusual facades and equally surprising interior design. In the Prada shop in New York, for example, you will find extravagant display technology with intelligent mirrors and magical light effects.

The lavish design of the stores is complemented by a whole range of technical innovations. Customers are automatically measured by a body scanner and can avail themselves of the services of virtual sales personnel if they desire.

Even more surprising innovations are to be found in the fitting rooms. As customers enter, a scanner automatically registers how many items they have brought with them. An additional display provides information on the fabrics, tips on the care of the garments, availability or special features. In addition, the central computer selects alternatives, for example matching shoes to go with a blouse. High-tech displays integrated in mirrors can show you what other garments would look like in combination with the item you are trying on. For example, the mirror can superimpose on your reflection images of various shoes at foot level, so there is no need to actually try them on to see how they look. You can have digital photos taken of yourself in the garments. These photos are stored on a server, and by simply pressing a button, you can take another look at yourself in the skirt you tried on before, without having to get changed again. The display shows the last garment you tried on, the mirror your current choice.

Design for services: Umpqua – what a bank!

In the field of services, differentiation through design is an even more important, if not the dominant, requirement, because services are not material. Immaterial things need to be given a material manifestation before they can become visible, communicable and identifiable to the customer. If the services you offer are boring and interchangeable with those of your competitors, you are neglecting the productive possibilities offered by design. The Umpqua bank from Oregon, which we mentioned in a previous chapter, focuses on the design factor to give it a competitive edge and a means of differentiating itself from the rest of the market. Umpqua is aware that customers are not really interested in how big their bank is, but rather in their own quality of life and in how far their bank can help them to boost it. The premises of the Umpqua bank, which have won numerous design awards, invite customers to linger. They can read the paper, have a cup of coffee, shop and of course, also do their banking there. Umpqua realized that it was up to it whether it made going to the bank a necessary evil for its customers, something to get done as quickly as possible, or alternatively a lifestyle decision. And so Umpqua does its best to make a visit to the bank a pleasurable experience. This is a very good example of a service enterprise taking advantage of design as a factor that wins not only prizes, but also the hearts of its customers, and differentiates it into the bargain.

Sales outlet design – not only for the final consumer

Companies tend to see sales outlet design exclusively as something that can be employed successfully in the consumer goods sector. But visit one of the large industrial trade fairs and you will see that in principle, exactly the same sort of thing goes on in the industrial goods sector. Many manufacturers achieve differentiation not only via the technology they offer but also increasingly through the design of their products, by establishing fields of aesthetic perception around their brand.

Business unconventionality box

Design is much more than just one step in the creation of a product, a step with the sole aim of making the product more aesthetically pleasing. Design gives you access to passion, emotion and identification and is the basis for emotional differentiation.

Business unconventionalists have understood that to be successful in future markets, you will have to ensure that your products and services stand out from the rest and are perceived as superior by the customer. Design has become a central factor in the struggle for differentiation, identification and customer loyalty. Take advantage of unusual design as a factor for achieving differentiation and success.

Remember the examples of Apple, BMW, Method and Kartell. They all illustrate how the design of products, packaging and sales outlets can become an integral part of corporate strategy.

Experience inside: create an experience, trigger emotions

Let us remain for a moment on the subject of differentiation. Business unconventionalists know that no matter how good your products are, how polite your staff are, how fast a service you provide, the customer could get most of what you have to offer from any number of competitors to be found in the Yellow Pages or via internet search engines.

There is only one way out, and it may seem disappointingly banal: do something new, be creative! Dare to try something completely new, something your competitors haven't even thought of. Your customers have to perceive your company, your products and services, as something different. Yet many companies simply haven't got the message yet. They waste a great deal of energy trying to score points with the customer by offering better quality, acquiring the best business location, by means of technological innovations and/or more efficient processes. They are convinced that they are better than their competitors and are sure that sooner or later, customers will realize this, too.

And so they rely on rational arguments illustrating why their products offer better performance, technology and quality than those of their competitors. But business unconventionalists add another factor to the mix, something that is rarely mentioned in connection with business life: emotions and experiences.

Rule 10 of business unconventionality

Experience inside: create an experience, trigger emotions.

Conventional thinking: you rely on rational argument and the persuasive power of your products (functionality, performance, quality etc) to win customers.

Business unconventionality: do something new, be creative. Add something more to the rational arguments, an element hardly ever talked about in the business environment: emotions and experiences. Use your services as a stage and your products as tools to help you win the hearts of your customers.

The mind justifies what the heart desires

Why do business unconventionalists believe in creating experiences? Because if you can package your offering as an experience for your customers, you will make it unforgettable and trigger emotions. Toys and dolls are probably the prime examples of products where the emotions of the customers are involved, yet how does the doll market 'tick'? The manufacturers of dolls focus on selling their products and accessories, while the actual 'experience' of playing with the dolls takes place predominantly at home.

Not so at American Girl Place. Here, customers enjoy the experience of play in the store itself. American Girl has two large establishments, the original branch in Chicago and another in New York. These are anything but typical toyshops. They offer the consumer a world of experience. The sale of products –American Girl dolls – is secondary here. Instead, customers old and young can enjoy a whole range of attractions – musical shows, cafés, restaurants, even a hairdressing salon for the dolls. Visitors can spend hundreds of dollars without buying a single doll. The special achievement of American Girl Place is that it has transferred the activity of playing from the nursery back into the store. And the concept is successful: with total sales of approximately 8 million dolls, American Girl ranks second after Barbie.

> Experiences are a fourth economic offering, as distinct from services as services are from goods.
>
> Joseph Pine and James Gilmore, *The Experience Economy*

Another example is the ice hotel in Jukkasjärvi in north Sweden. Every winter, the hotel is rebuilt from ice. The beds are made of ice, with coverings of reindeer skin and sleeping bags. The furniture, the crockery, the glasses – everything is made of ice. And although the average temperature is below zero, guests from all over the world come and pay over €200 a night to stay there.

Really cool: the ice hotel

What is the product this hotel is selling? Is it the fact that you sleep on reindeer skins? Or that you can enjoy a drink in a bar made of ice? The breathtaking view over the snow-covered landscape of north Sweden? Or is it everything together, the whole package? The product is all these things – and much more. A night spent at the ice hotel may soon be over, but the experience is unforgettable, the memory of each little detail and the special atmosphere in this most short-lived of hotel stays. It is an experience far beyond a mere journey, a good night's sleep and good food.

Following the Swedish example, a new 'icebar' has now opened in Milan. The Absolut Icebar in the centre of the Italian metropolis is made entirely of ice – walls, bar and tables, even the glasses. The temperature inside the bar is five degrees below zero, so guests are handed moon boots and thermal coats at the entrance.

The bar needs complete reconstruction every six months. The 60 tons of ice required every month to maintain the bar, which has an area of 120 square metres, are flown in directly from Sweden. And the bar serves only vodka – to be drunk on the rocks, of course.

Experiences in business-to-business: computer nerds

You can create experiences to ensure added value and differentiation in the consumer goods industry, but the concept can also be applied

Figure 3.9 Some like it cool – the Ice Hotel in Jukkasjärvi
Source: Icehotel AB

successfully in the B2B sector. The examples we shall look at here are an IT service company, a producer of construction machinery, a manufacturer of air-conditioning technology and a hotel that specializes in organizing events for companies.

Let us start by taking a look at US IT specialists Geek Squad. If the name conjures up pictures of people who talk to their computers, wear glasses with lenses as thick as bottle glass, live on a basic diet of coke and pizza and can only be persuaded to leave their chairs in emergencies, you would be wrong.

This is a company that has cleverly managed to turn a very undifferentiated service, a service that is provided by numerous other companies in every town and city, into an extremely successful business idea. It has done so by staging an experience. As a service provider, Geek Squad supports companies when their IT networks have crashed, when printers refuse to work, files cannot be opened or computers start making funny noises. In a creative mix of humour,

Figure 3.10 Geek Squad – dark sunglasses, black suits: the IT special agents

Source: Best Buy Stores LP, www.geeksquad.com

innovation and the creation of a special experience, the company has turned itself into a team of troubleshooting 'special agents' to help customers solve computer problems. Geek Squad employees wear white shirts with narrow black ties, white socks and black trousers. They carry a 'Special Agent' badge and look just like Jack and Elwood Blues in the legendary film *The Blues Brothers*.

The company has successfully turned a relatively unglamorous service into an experience for the customer. And what has it gained? Strong differentiation from other companies in the field, a lot of free word-of-mouth advertising, a certain cult status and an extremely successful business.

Business clients are looking for an experience, and men will be boys!

Geek Squad is a good example of a B2B company that has successfully differentiated itself by adding an experience and an element of fun to its purely functional offering.

> I see us as being in the art business. Art, entertainment and mobile sculpture, which, coincidentally, happens to provide transportation
>
> Bob Lutz, Vice Chairman of General Motors

This example also shows that following the crowd is not always a wise idea. In a marketplace where everyone is scrabbling for the crumbs, companies can only differentiate and compete on price. Try a completely different strategic approach! Set out to be different!

More and more companies in the B2B markets are discovering that the creation of an experience can be the way to economic success. Whereas the focus here is mainly on the product with all its technical details, on utility and price–performance ratios, unconventional thinkers have realized that producers of industrial goods can achieve true differentiation and innovation by packaging their offerings as an experience.

One example of such a company is US construction machinery producer Case. The company runs the Case Tomahawk Experience Center in Wisconsin. Here, customers can try out excavators and bulldozers to their heart's content. The whole experience is a real event: Who didn't dream of driving an excavator when they were a child? And now that childhood dream can come true! Case also organizes competitions where customers and potential customers compete against each other in digging, shovelling and levelling events.

But that is only one aspect of Case's clever strategy. Case invites both financial decision makers (managing directors, owners and so on) and users (supervisors, bulldozer operators, etc) from companies that are potential customers to try out the equipment together. It needs the boss to be there, because he or she is the one who will make the final decision on whether to buy. But the boss is seldom the person who actually operates the machinery. The user, on the other hand, is in a much better position to appreciate why machinery from Case is the best. Once the user is convinced, he or she will help sell the Case products to the boss.

Case is an impressive example of how events can be used very successfully in B2B markets. No matter how many glossy brochures you distribute among your sales personnel, and no matter how good they are at explaining the technical features of your construction machinery to potential customers at their premises, nothing can compare with the advantages of entertaining potential customers on your own ground and offering them the unique experience of trying out the equipment for themselves.

Experiencing invisible technology

In principle, any company can stage an experience in its showrooms – even if the product is something as unspectacular as facility management systems. You have to admit that this is the last product you would class as 'supersexy', and yet it can still be turned into an experience. And the company that consistently does just that is Johnson Controls in Milwaukee.

At the headquarters of the company, staff have set up the Brengel Technology Center as a showcase for the Johnson Controls range of air-conditioning and building automation technology. The centre, which has won numerous awards is a showcase for air-conditioning. The goal: to convince customers of the importance of the right air-conditioning system installed in their new buildings.

The Nortel Executive Briefing Center in the Research Triangle Park in North Carolina is another example of a user-oriented experience centre in the B2B sector. On arrival, guests are issued with a smart card which allows them personal and interactive access to the Nortel technologies. The Center offers cutting-edge technology, including Virtual Reality Labs where guests can view presentations tailored to their individual requirements. This allows them to experience at first hand how Nortel technologies can play a central role in their lives.

Reinforcing the effect of the event: Scalaria shows the way

The examples of Nortel Networks and Johnson Controls have shown how companies can stage experiences in their showrooms. But how can an entire company become a world of experience? To see this, we need to turn our attention to Austria, to Lake Wolfgang. Former German Chancellor Helmut Kohl spent his holidays by this lake in the Salzkammergut area for many years. It has even been suggested that the lake should be rechristened Lake Helmut Kohl in his honour, but that's a different story.

We are going to look at a hotel on Lake Wolfgang, a hotel where, as far as we know, Helmut Kohl has never stayed. This is no typical tourist hotel. Instead, it specializes in the organization of conferences, meetings and seminars for big corporations. Hotel Scalaria has positioned itself successfully by offering a unique experience, and that in a market overcrowded with good, reliable establishments all offering an inviting ambience and top service. The owner says, 'We have no competition. I have created a completely new niche.' Even the welcoming words on the hotel's website (www.scalaria.com) are unusual:

> Thank you for visiting the event resort, the unique location for corporate events and product shows. Enjoy the fascinating moments from our world and then succumb to the charms surrounding stage, show and wow effects ...

Need we say more? Hotel Scalaria sets a whole new standard with its focus on events. And a look at the guest book reveals just how successful the concept is: Scalaria has organized events for Allianz, Bentley, Breitling, Canon, DaimlerChrysler, Dior, EON, Escada, Ferrari, Giorgio Armani, Gucci and Hugo Boss. What does the Scalaria have to do with business unconventionality? Everything! While traditional business thinking leads companies to focus on aspects like friendly and quick service, reliability and the price–performance ratio, business unconventionalists choose a different approach. They acknowledge the importance of these aspects, while at the same time they are aware that all other companies on the market are focusing on them. Thus the only way to achieve true differentiation and unique status is to do something completely different, in this case by creating an experience for the customer.

Using experiences to cement bonds

The skilful creation of unique experiences anchors brands in the minds of (potential) customers. And creating experiences is a good way to establish a deeper bond between a company and its customers. As a consequence, experiences play an increasing role in the communication between a company and its customers, in both the industrial goods and the consumer goods sectors, as many target groups can only be reached by means of emotional, entertainment-oriented instruments. Creating a unique experience can boost a company's credibility, which will ideally extend to its products and increase brand loyalty.

One word of caution: When you engage in event marketing, be careful not to let your event degenerate into a huge publicity show. Offer your customers real value.

> Brand capital has nothing to do with marketing... but with the emotional attachment of consumers to the brand.
>
> Howard Schultz, chairman and chief strategist,
> Starbucks Coffee Company

Creating atmosphere: take an anthropological walk

Even if many companies use the word 'experience' in a very broad sense, many things that are advertised as experiences are in fact not experiences at all. An amusing anecdote on this topic: while staying at the Radisson SAS Hotel in Erfurt recently, we read about the new spa area of the hotel. The brochure advertised its 'adventure showers' as a special highlight. We were of course disrespectful enough to ask what sort of adventure one might have under the shower in the hotel spa. Unfortunately, the management couldn't throw any light on the matter.

But back to the subject of experiences. Taking a stroll through an oriental bazaar, move on to an English country mansion and finally buy some Spanish pottery, and all in just one hour? Impossible? But this is precisely the business idea behind Anthropologie, a US store chain. Its outlets offer an unusual range of products including not only clothing but also the furniture and accessories with which the stores are decorated.

Shopping at Anthropologie is like walking through a flea market, a trip through different worlds. Fluffy bathrobes are displayed on huge four-poster beds piled high with cushions – and next to the bed, you will find picture frames decorated with shells, like those made by artisans on Majorca. The main target group is urban women with a higher income between the ages of 20 and 60. Anthropologie clearly differentiates itself from other, more youth-oriented companies. However, that doesn't mean that you will find trousers with elasticated waists, aprons or similar trappings of a conservative nature here. The products on sale range from low-price items costing US$2 to original objets d'art for US$2,000.

Anthropologie has more than 50 stores in the United States. On average, customers spend an amazing 1.5 hours in the store – despite the fact that Anthropologie does not advertise in the conventional sense. According to Glen Senk, head of the company, 'One of our core philosophies is that we spend the money that other companies spend on marketing to create a store experience that exceeds people's expectations. We invest not in advertising slogans, but in the realization of our philosophy.'

And the concept is relatively simple: do not only offer your customers your products, but create unique experiences around them. With the range of products on the market becoming ever more homogenous, creating experiences is a good way to differentiate yourself. The borders between art and commerce become fluid.

Experiences outside opening hours: the bookstore with more

With more than 50 branches in the United States, Anthropologie is not really one of the small fish on the market. But can companies with a staff of only 8 or 10 afford to offer their customers a unique experience? Wouldn't you need the budget of a bigger company to do that?

It is possible on a restricted budget! You don't have to hire top designers to offer your customers carefully orchestrated and unique experiences that leave a lasting impression and have the potential to keep customers loyal to you over the long term. The Deuerlich book-

Figure 3.11 Anthropologie – the de luxe flea market
Source: Anthropologie – the de luxe flea market

store in Göttingen, Germany, is proof that small and medium-sized enterprises can also profit from event marketing. Under the slogan 'Midsummer night in Pippi Longstocking's Villa Villekula', the bookstore invited customers young and old to an evening event in the store. There were readings from the best-known works of Swedish author Astrid Lindgren, and Swedish snacks and beverages were served throughout the night. Anyone who nodded off could spend the night there, and breakfast was served for those who were still there next morning.

The customers paid a small entrance fee, with the night divided into four sessions. They could book individual sessions or for the whole night, including a place to sleep. The initiators were very satisfied with the results. The resonance was so great that many customers have asked when Deuerlich plans to hold its next book night.

This is an excellent example of how medium-sized companies can take advantage of the trend towards event marketing with the help of creativity and commitment, and on a low budget. The example teaches us something else, too. You are only selling your customers a business

Figure 3.12   Deuerlich – creative new ideas on a shoestring budget
Source: Sebastian Mauritz, Deuerlich Books & Media

proposition when you ask them to pay for it. In the case of experiences, this means charging an entrance fee. No matter how thrilling the experience you create around your product or service, you are only offering an economic value if, like a concert agency, you sell tickets.

Business unconventionality box

It was never our intention to enter the transport industry. We are still in the entertainment industry – at an altitude of 25,000 feet.

Richard Branson, head of the Virgin Group,
founder of the Virgin Atlantic airline

Richard Branson's comment on the USP of his airline can be applied to many other industries. Remember the ice hotel in North Sweden, construction machinery producers Case, which boosts sales with the help of unique experiences, and the Geek Squad, an IT services company that has managed, through humour and the skilful creation of a unique experience, to turn a company operating in a largely undifferentiated competitive environment into a successful business venture.

Do something new, be creative. Add an additional element to the rational arguments you use to sell your products and services, an element that is rarely mentioned in connection with business activities: emotions and experiences. Use your services as a stage and your products as tools to win the hearts of your customers.

Easy Inc: offer clarity, cut out the frills to make your product irresistible

- Number of functions Mercedes-Benz removed from its cars because drivers didn't need them or didn't know how to use them: 600.
- Height of the stack of information produced by each inhabitant of the Earth per year, in metres: 9.
- Number of pieces of information reaching every one of us every day between the time we get up and the time we go to bed: 10,000.
- Probability that, straight after a news programme, German television viewers will have already forgotten what they have just seen: one in three.
- Number of consumer articles on the market in Europe: approximately 400,000.
- Number of consumer articles bought on average by a European household: 350.

(source: *Brand Eins* magazine)

Too much information, too many functions, too many goods and services available – is it any wonder that average consumers are out of their depth? And what do companies do? They make sure that things keep on getting more and more complicated. Or do you still compare all the tariffs offered by the various mobile phone companies? No? Then you're in pretty good company, because many people don't. And what do the phone companies do? They invent yet another price model to add to the already impenetrable maze. Or just remember the last time you bought a digital camera or a DVD player. By the time you have finished comparing all the products on the market, a new model has been launched. And before you've even learnt how to operate it properly, it's time to get the next one. And the friendly salesperson in your local electrical goods store? While you are standing in front of the shelves, scratching your head and hoping to get some helpful advice, he or she simply reads you the product description off the box and hopes that this invaluable professional advice will help you make up your mind fast.

Simplify

Customers are way out of their depth. The world is full of confusing data, information, services and products – and their number increases every day. Customers are sick of this senseless jungle of products and services, and they are no longer willing to waste their precious time navigating their way around the artificial distinctions between products that often offer not 'more' but 'more of the same'.

> In the next few years, what we will be increasingly striving for is simplification. We need more simplification in communication, in presentation, in our products. Fewer components. Simpler design. Companies tend to complicate everything – life tends to get more complicated.
>
> Jack Welch, former Chairman of General Electric

Business unconventionalists have realized that the key to success lies not in creating more complexity but in reducing complexity for the consumer. This engenders a feeling of security and trust, which in turn cements the relationship between seller and buyer.

Rule 11 of business unconventionality

Easy Inc: offer clarity, cut out the frills to make your product irresistible.

Conventional thinking: you keep on expanding the range of products and services you offer and introducing even more price models. Your aim: to ensure that the customers have an ever-increasing range and variety of products and services to choose from.
Business unconventionality: you cut out the frills, simplify, focus on the essentials. Offer clarity and simplicity that your customers will not be able to resist!

The reduction of complexity does not mean making everything simple. Simple would imply the removal of complexity instead of making it more easily comprehensible. The reduction of complexity means focusing on the essentials, the art of cutting out the frills.

But how can you achieve clarity and simplicity in your range of products and services? Well, complexity manifests itself in four areas where you can take action:

- **Range of products and services**: reducing the range to make it easier for customers to make their selection.
- **Price model**: no jungle of different pricing systems (see the telephone companies), but instead a clear and comprehensible price structure that guarantees a fair price–performance ratio.
- **Interaction**: simplifying the operation of the products.
- **Communication**: easily comprehensible and clear communication with customers, business partners etc and within the company (with staff).

In this section, we shall concentrate on the first of these points. It should not be forgotten, however, that you need to turn all the screws at once to ensure a maximum of simplification. If you keep these points in mind while reading through the other sections, you will see the principle of simplification at work in many of the examples we describe.

An easier choice: the jam experiment

A study carried out by US scientists Sheena Iyengar and Mark Leppler showed that the number of customers who actually buy is much higher when the range of products on offer is not so wide and confusing. They analysed customers' reactions to larger and smaller selections, and discovered that if there were 64 different jams to choose from, 60 per cent of customers stopped to examine the range, but only 3 per cent of them actually bought, whereas if the range of jams was reduced to six, only 40 per cent of customers stopped to look, but of those 40 per cent, 30 per cent bought some jam. In other words, six times more customers bought from the limited range than from the much wider range of 64 different jams. Customers find larger ranges confusing: they become disoriented, can't make up their minds, find the choice stressful and frustrating.

Stores with a limited and attractive selection of products have been the winners in the last few years. What they have in common is that they offer a clear, straightforward range, easy for customers to find their way around. No unlimited choice, no confusing array of different prices. The winners are stores or brands that don't confuse the customer with unlimited choice, endless variety and constantly changing offers, but instead provide orientation and clear, focused offerings, often with surprisingly good price–performance ratios. Think credible, stable, dependable; quality you can rely on; prices you can rely on. In Germany, customers of the successful discount chain Aldi don't need to compare prices, because for years now they have seen that Aldi's prices are very low. In this way, Aldi has established a relationship based on trust with its customers, and trust ensures less complexity.

More than coffee: the Tchibo system

'A new world every week' is Tchibo's motto, and it applies this motto 52 times a year. Every week it presents a miniature product universe which exists for just seven days and comprises up to 40 articles under the company's own brand name TCM. The range is tailored so precisely to the requirements of consumers that they often wonder how Tchibo knows them so well. Tchibo always seems to have just the things that you were thinking of replacing – a new soap dispenser for the bathroom, wellington boots for gardening or a new barbecue for the patio. And each product is available in just one design, so there is no problem making up your mind.

As a 'temporary specialist trader', Tchibo sells more of each article in Germany than all the other companies in the sector put together. The group's annual turnover has increased by 8 per cent to €3.3 million, while German retailers as a whole have sustained losses of 2 per cent. And an even more surprising fact: the Hamburg-based company now makes a higher turnover with its selection of goods and services that changes every week than with the coffee that is its core offering.

This is only possible with the help of a perfect logistics system, skilful product planning and rigorous quality management. The result: customers can rely on getting low prices and good quality – and all this with a limited range of products. This creates trust and familiarity because the system is based on continuity and stability. And this in turn boosts customer loyalty and cements the bond between supplier and buyer, because reliability is a value important to the customer.

> Customers no longer want 10 metres of shelving packed with so many different yoghurts that their eyes hurt trying to take them all in. What people long for is a reassuringly predictable world they can trust implicitly.
>
> Stephan Grünewald,
> managing director of market research institute Rheingold in Cologne

The success of Tchibo's concept is not the only evidence that customers want less complexity. Just take a look at the bestseller lists. *Simplify your Life*, published in October 2001, has sold over 350,000 copies in Germany alone. Worldwide, more than a million people who want to reduce complexity and simplify their lives have bought it.

Less is more: Unilever thins out its range

The success of Aldi has made it clear to everyone that focusing on the essentials can work miracles for your sales figures. Market and consumer research experts agree that there is more to the success of Aldi and similar stores than just the hype of cheap products. It is based on a development that business unconventionalists have long recognized and used to their advantage: fewer products mean better sales. The giants among the consumer goods producers have now woken up to the trend. They have made radical cuts in their portfolios. Dutch-British conglomerate Unilever (which has brands such as Iglo, Knorr, Sunil, Coral) has banished 75 per cent of its products from the portfolio over the last four years – a total of 1,200 products.

To quote Stephan Grünewald again, 'People long for much less complexity. They need clarity and control to counteract the general uncertainty in their lives.' For companies, this means straightforward product ranges, products with clearly defined utility, focusing on the most important sales channels and simple, transparent price structures.

Reducing complexity in the price model: Budget shows you how

Simple and transparent price structures should be a given in any company that has at least a vague idea of what customer orientation means, but reality tells a different story. One example is German railways. In October 2002, Deutsche Bahn chairman Mehdorn was

Figure 3.13   Unilever slims down its portfolio
Source: Unilever

confident of success: 'We aim to be the best railway company in Europe, among other things with the help of our new price system.' But when the new price system was introduced, it quickly became clear that this was an illusion. It wasn't the customers. They hadn't suddenly mutated to idiots incapable of understanding the new tariffs. It was the complexity of the system itself that caused tremendous problems. And in the light of this, Deutsche Bahn's vow to give customers more clarity with the new price structures seemed particularly ironic.

That was the theory. In practice, long queues formed at the ticket offices and the most common comments heard from travellers were 'Idiocy' and 'Shameless'. And as usual, it wasn't the people responsible for the chaos who bore the brunt of customers' dissatisfaction, but the Deutsche Bahn employees manning the ticket offices and the trains. In the midst of all this confusion, there was a clearly bewildered Deutsche Bahn management that had introduced the new system with the aim of providing greater clarity. Since that disastrous launch, the new system has been revised and made more easily comprehensible. But it is surely legitimate to ask why on earth a company would introduce a price system it has not fully understood itself, which in some cases proved too much for its own computer systems to handle, and under which any deviation from the standard request for 'a return ticket to ...' causes major problems?

Yet the solution is so easy. You can score points with the customers by introducing simple and transparent price structures. Car-rental company Budget got it right. Can you remember the last time you searched the internet for a low car-rental rate? Most companies have extremely complicated rates that create more confusion than clarity. Even after long and intensive internet research, consumers can never be sure that they have really got the best rate available – and that means stress.

Conventional thinking leads to most of the companies happily chiming in and adding their own contribution to the cat-and-mouse game they play with the customers by trying to woo them with even more complicated rates. Clever business unconventionalists, on the other hand, are aware that customers are both not stupid enough to fall for that old trick, and increasingly irritated by the complexity of the price models. Simplifying and streamlining them is becoming a more and more convincing sales argument.

Car-rental firm Budget provides an impressive example of how reducing the complexity of the price models creates true added value for customers. While other rental companies offer customers the choice between hundreds of different rates and almost as many different tariff models, Budget Germany has only two rates: Economy and Business. For €39 and €59 respectively, the customer can hire a car in the desired class with unlimited mileage and comprehensive insurance. The advantage for consumers: the highest possible degree of transparency, and no wasted time spent searching for the best rate. And no confusion, because customers know exactly what they are getting for their money.

> It irritates people that the truth is so simple. They forget that it will be difficult enough for them to apply it.
>
> Johann Wolfgang von Goethe

Simplicity as a corporate philosophy

However, just simplifying the price model or taking a few products out of the range is not enough to reduce complexity. Simplicity is a corporate philosophy that begins during the development of new products (simplicity of use as the commanding principle) and permeates all ensuing processes: a clear advertising message, clearly delineated aims and responsibilities, customer orientation in all departments and a sales organization that rigorously cuts out unnecessary distribution channels.

But back to the reduction of complexity for the user. It is a fact that in many cases, modern-day products are difficult to use. Just think of cars that are so full of complicated technology that as a driver, you have to wade your way through a 200-page manual before you even dare to turn the ignition key. Or think of your mobile phone. Many mobile phone users despair of ever finding their way around the endless functions of their phones when they haven't even mastered the simplest basic operations. And have you ever tried to buy a train ticket from a ticket machine? Either the machine is for tickets to local destinations and you have to enter the appropriate code to select your desired destination, or – even more of a nightmare – you have to struggle with a touch screen that insists on triggering any function except the one you pressed.

Conventional thinking dictates that everyone must join in the race to incorporate cutting-edge technologies and pack as many functions as possible into their products. Business unconventionality tells us: simplify use by making the products self-explanatory.

There are many examples of simple ideas for making products easier to use:

- beer bottles with crown caps that can be opened without a bottle opener by simply turning them;
- deep-frozen pizza bases which come already rolled out on their own piece of baking paper;
- mobile phones with only the basic functions for senior citizens;
- instant noodles: just add hot water and they're ready to eat;
- 'Swiffer' household cleaning equipment, which has even the most unwilling people happily cleaning the parquet flooring;
- washing machines that automatically select the appropriate wash cycle;
- the simple and easy-to-use graphic user interface of the first Macintosh computers from Apple, which had a decisive influence on the way all modern PC operating systems work;
- the menu of Nokia mobiles, which are subjected to intensive usability tests to ensure that they are as simple as possible and easy to grasp without lengthy instruction: Nokia has set a worldwide standard that has been adopted by most of its competitors.

Sense and simplicity

A short time ago, Dutch electronics group Philips replaced its original slogan 'Let's make things better' with the new motto 'Sense and simplicity', with 'sense' standing for sensible and purposeful and 'simplicity' for simple and consumer-friendly.

Philips realized that consumers want products that are simple and easy to use. Just think of the Philips Senseo coffee machine, which only has three buttons; an on-off switch and two others to select the desired number of cups. 'Simplicity' is the new key word at Philips. 'We want people to perceive Philips as the company that makes modern technology easy to understand – a simple and easy experience,' says Andrea Ragnetti, chief marketing officer.

More and more companies are realizing that consumers are overwhelmed by the ever-growing flood of complicated new technologies when what they are looking for is exactly the opposite: they do want new technology, but not at the price of diminished user-friendliness. In order to give consumers what they want, you must be willing to

Figure 3.14 Technology can't be simple enough – Philips knows!
Source: Philips Austria GmbH

question yourself constantly. Do we really need this new feature or is there a simpler way? Would there be something missing if we simply left it out? These are the core questions that need to be asked every time a new product is developed. Because only by having the courage to cut the superfluous details will you be able to create user-friendly products – and cut costs into the bargain.

Business unconventionality box

It takes a scholar to say simple things in a complicated way and a wise man to say complicated things in an easy way.

Charles Tschopp, Swiss author

Aldi points the way! Tchibo shows how you can operate extremely successfully as a 'temporary specialist trader' with a limited number of products. Budget scores points with the consumer with a radically simplified price system. Create clarity and cut the frills to create products and services your customers will find irresistible.

4 Different thinking: price

Some authors suggest that what people want above all else is low prices and that for consumers, price has become the simplest and most reliable way of deciding which product to buy. In their opinion, 'cheap' has become synonymous with 'good'. But is it really true that companies have no other choice but to cut their prices even further? Is it true that cheap is good and even cheaper even better?

We don't think so. We are convinced that you shouldn't be wasting your energy trying to find a way to undercut your competitors' prices by 1 or 2 per cent. That is hardly creative, and it's wearing in the long run. You only need to look at the German food retailers to see exactly how unproductive it is. For years now, there has been the same discouraging situation: cut-throat competition and sluggish demand have reduced profit margins to below 1 per cent in some cases. Most decision makers in the market seem helpless to do anything about it. All they can come up with is restructuring and cost cutting drives. But this is not a solution, because if you can think up a way to cut costs, however marginally, your competitors are only going to follow suit immediately. The answer? Question the truth of statements like 'There's no other way' or 'Everyone's doing it', and glean inspiration from other industries and other countries.

Of course it's only human to look in familiar places for solutions to our problems. If everyone else is cutting back on staff, we are definitely not going to fly in the face of the trend and start hiring. If our competitors are all convinced that the only way to win customers is to offer low prices and free additional services, we are not going to dare to ask our customers to pay for them. We naturally feel much more at ease on familiar ground. And we are convinced that if we only watch the competition closely enough, we will find a solution to all our problems.

But – and the examples in the preceding chapters have illustrated this – not one of the business unconventionalists we mentioned has achieved success by following this strategy. They all looked not to familiar ground but to entirely different industries for answers, and they all consistently and repeatedly challenged the status quo. They didn't accept statements like 'That's just how it is in our industry.' There is a lesson to be learnt here! Look over the rim of your teacup and combine the familiar with the unusual.

Ikea's Ingvar Kamprad was able to offer his furniture at unbeatably low prices because he bought cheaply and delegated part of the work (transport and assembly of the furniture) to his customers, and not because he cut back his staff to a painful minimum. Michael Dell offers his customers good products at low prices because he turned the conventional business model for his industry upside down by selling exclusively to the consumer. Products are configured to customer requirements after receipt of the order. A very clever idea, because it means Dell builds computers for its customers and uses their money to do so. So you see, it can work! Business unconventionality means cleverness, which in turn is a combination of the following elements: curiosity, enthusiasm and the courage to do things differently.

Competing for customers on price? No!

In their search for customers, companies employ an effective but extremely dangerous weapon: the lowest price. It may win you customers, but you are going to lose them again just as quickly when your rivals undercut your prices by a few cents. The second problem: profit margins dwindle, and you have to start cutting costs if you want to make any profit at all. But for most companies, cutting back on personnel is just not feasible any more. As the Germans say, you can't pick the pockets of a naked man – so there's no point in trying to reduce costs even further!

> How will we know when we're done restructuring? Where is the dividing line between cutting fat and cutting muscle?
>
> Gary Hamel, business strategist

Don't get us wrong. Restructuring and cost-cutting programmes are sensible and important measures, but they simply correct the mistakes that were made in the past. They won't equip a company to survive in future markets. They are no substitute for sound strategy and a clear plan for the future. Any company that introduces the most stringent cost-cutting programmes but neglects to secure future markets is going to find itself in a vicious circle, constantly on the run from steadily dwindling margins.

The logical conclusion is that it's not enough simply to undercut your competitors' prices by a couple of percentage points. Why? Because, as strategy guru Michael Porter puts it, price cuts are usually 'suicide', as your rivals can easily cut their prices to the same level. The same applies to cutting costs. These are very short-term solutions, as the other companies on the market will simply follow suit.

The long-term view: escaping the price trap

So how do business unconventionalists solve the problem? What do they do to escape the vicious circle of price cuts and shrinking margins? First and foremost, they focus on the long-term objectives. This is very important. Never let the pressure of day-to-day business life distract you from the essentials. Panicking and reacting to your competitors' price cuts by trying to cut your costs even further only creates the illusion that you are in control of the situation – and is hardly likely to lead to any lasting innovation.

You must take the time to think things through. Ponder, brainstorm and think constantly about what unconventional route you could take. If you can manage to come up with a price model that flies in the face of the established conventions in your industry, you might find that this has promising consequences: It could give you a temporary monopoly, access to a completely new market, a learning infrastructure ensuring you get a competitive edge in the development of new products and services for a whole new generation of customers – and of course, sales growth and profit margins that will please not only you but also your investors.

> If you have no clear, hard-to-imitate and continually provable competitive edge, you are doomed to competing on price. And the pressure on prices will increase, above all where products are very similar and therefore interchangeable. If you have a unique proposition, you won't have this problem! So, make your company unique!
>
> Klaus Kobjoll, German hotel owner, author and trainer

This is what we mean by being consistently *different* and consistently *smart*. It's not a question of undercutting your competitors' prices at all costs, but of establishing a lasting advantage in price structure. But that is not the only possible route: you could also challenge the established price model in your industry or radically simplify it, like car-hire firm Budget, which managed to double its market share in just three months. And you must ensure that your customers perceive you as different. Because if you can escape the uniform market with its uniform offerings, your customers will be only too willing to pay for the privilege of acquiring a unique product or service.

Ask the price question: do it now!

It's worth thinking hard about the question of price., but this book is not about providing you with a recipe for cost-cutting programmes enabling you to reduce your prices by 0.5 per cent or woo customers with generous discounts. We want to apply the cleverness of business unconventionality to the subject of price and see how it might help us.

The following examples illustrate that price management need not be complicated. So just forget about demand-oriented price creation with the help of the price–performance quotient or the hedonic pricing method for a minute. Approach the question of price cleverly and creatively. Being creative doesn't mean you have to reinvent the wheel. New ideas are literally all around you. All you have to do is discover them and adapt them to your own situation. Or, in the words of Chinese philosopher Lao Tse, 'To perceive things is the germ of intelligence.'

As we said, you don't have to reinvent the wheel here – you only have to look at the fish buffet at Ikea, where a meal costs just a few cents, to see that – but be careful, you pay by weight. Most other dishes in the Ikea restaurants are at fixed prices, but there are also some 'All you can eat!' special offers. The difference is in the mix!

In other words: You need clever pricing! Discounts and competition-driven price cuts are not the solution – what you need is business unconventionality!

Price DNA: question the established price models

The classic mindset never questions the established basis for pricing in an industry: petrol prices are quoted per litre, apples are priced according to weight, cucumbers are priced per unit, wine per bottle. Lawyers are paid according to the amount in dispute or charge hourly fees, consultants charge per day. Although Moses didn't come back down Mount Sinai clutching tablets of stone with defined price models for individual industries, the rules are seemingly irrefutable. And neither producers nor customers question them. Challenging the established price models for an industry means thinking the unthinkable – and then trying it out.

Rule 12 of business unconventionality

Price DNA: question the established price models.

Conventional thinking: you take the established price model for your industry as a given and strive for optimization within these limits.
Business unconventionality: instead of wasting your energy trying to optimize the established price model for your industry or to be just that little bit cheaper than your competitors, you create your own price model.

Wouldn't it be an interesting idea to calculate the price of a car based on its weight? A kilo of Smart for €12 or a kilo of Mercedes E class for €21? Absurd, you say? Perhaps it is, but it is just such unusual ideas that may reveal the potential for differentiation and innovation. Sometimes you need to break with tradition to find new business ideas.

Business unconventionalists choose unusual routes. Instead of optimizing the established price model, they create their own. And the following examples show you how this is possible.

Creating your own price model: consultation at a monthly flat rate

The IBF – Institut für Betriebsführung AG – provides consulting services to medium-sized enterprises. Instead of the usual hourly or daily rates for its services, it charges a flat monthly rate based on the size of the client's workforce. This flat rate covers all services rendered by the IBF within that month.

From the clients' point of view, this is a very good idea, as they know what they will be paying at the end of the month and don't get any nasty surprises when they receive a fat bill from their consultants. And for this monthly payment, they can consult any of IBF's pool of experts, specialists on business management, marketing, pensions, personnel or financing, without having to conclude a separate consultancy contract each time. All in all, this solution is more convenient for medium-sized enterprises.

The system works in IBF's favour, too. Customer loyalty is high, and they can easily project profits for the coming months. The overheads for project calculation and invoicing are also significantly lower than with the traditional price model. And the consultants profit from the satisfaction of their clients, who find the system 'fair'. By the way, this is not a new idea! Many large-scale enterprises pay external consultants a flat rate for specified services. Only services outside this framework are billed individually. But here, conditions have to be renegotiated constantly, whereas the IBF model applies to all customers and all projects.

What about your industry? Could you replace individual billing with a flat rate? What would that mean for your clients and for your company?

Dodging the competition: simple but effective!

The example of IBF shows one other important thing: when we talk about questioning the established price models, it's not always a question of differentiation from the rest of the field, but often of simply dodging the competition. The idea is that instead of competing head-on on price, you simply move the playing field, because differentiation from your competitors is the only way to achieve strong long-term positioning.

How to set about it? First, you have to define the established price model for your industry. What models and unwritten rules apply? The next step is to take that price model apart, examine its individual components, try replacing them, adding to them, changing them and then put the whole thing back together. Our next example shows one way to do it.

New sources of income through mixed financing

You want to put an ad in the newspaper, for example to sell your old kitchen? Then you will pay a fixed price calculated on the basis of the length of the ad, the circulation of the paper and whether it is a local, regional or national paper. If you want to put a classified ad in the paper, you bear the costs – that's the way it is!

But there is an alternative! Papers like *Bazar*, *Sperrmüll* and *Zweite Hand* have challenged this established price model. Private individuals can place ads free of charge, and the paper is financed partly through the trade advertisements it carries and primarily through the price of the paper itself.

This type of mixed financing is often found in the media sector. In the last few years, private radio and television stations have found new sources of income. For example, quiz programmes where listeners or viewers can phone in on expensive charge lines and win prizes have not only become a familiar and popular feature, but also contribute to financing the operation of the station. What the consumer perceives as an additional service, interactive radio or television, is above all a lucrative source of income for the station, and the model is gaining in importance as revenues from advertising fall.

Who foots the bill? Not your customer

There are other ways to break with the established price model for your industry. Either you can charge customers the full amount, or you can charge them a part of it. And who will pay the rest? Find sponsors to bear a large part of the costs. This, for example, is the innovative price model of an Austrian car-rental company. The idea: customers can hire a car for just €1 a day. The 'trick'? The company's fleet of rental cars, all Smarts, are travelling billboards intended to be seen by as many people as possible. The company's main source of income is the companies that hire the cars as an advertising medium.

The brain behind the company is none other than former racing driver, pilot and entrepreneur Niki Lauda. And Lauda Motion all started with the simple question: Who says the customer always has to pay? It's not dictated by any law. The next step was to find someone to bear the costs. An interesting feature is that the customer hiring the car has to drive it a minimum number of kilometres per day to ensure that enough people see the advertising.

Figure 4.1   Billboards on wheels – the €1 Smart
Source: Lauda Car.com Mobile Advertising GmbH, www.laudamotion.com

Lauda Motion shows how price models that are unusual for an industry can provide a means of differentiation and innovation. That's why it can be such a rewarding exercise to think about the conventional price models in other industries and try to transfer them to your own to see whether you can use them as an interesting innovation.

And of course, Lauda Motion is not in direct competition with Budget or Sixt, as it has completely different target groups. Businesspeople are unlikely to want to travel to their next important appointment in a Smart that has been converted into a billboard on wheels and then have to drive around the block a few times to get the required number of kilometres on the clock. On the other hand, if you're a smart shopper looking for a good deal, you're hardly likely to rent an Audi A6 from Budget.

The ultimate in pricing: free of charge

An innovative mixed financing model is the idea behind the fleet of Smarts, which is financed through advertising – the price the customer pays is of purely symbolic value. Our next example is about a similar experiment in price calculation, but in a somewhat different market. Open-source operating system Linux is revolutionizing the software industry with its free software. But where do the distributors and the computer retailers earn their money if the product is free?

In the classic price model, software is licensed. An Office or Windows licence has to be purchased from Microsoft for each workstation or CPU. The more users, the more the customer has to pay for the licence. And then there are the updates and upgrades the customer has to buy. Linux is different. You can download Linux software from the internet and install it as many times as you like. Linux also offers regular updates, and these too are free of charge. Yet some companies make good money with Linux and other freeware. How?

They earn their money with services. Distributors put together various freeware packages, all coordinated, develop simple installation routines and offer their packages for sale as their own Linux distributions with additional manuals. This is very convenient for customers, who don't need to spend time coordinating the software themselves. Companies also earn a lot of money with Linux seminars, consulting services and individual profiling. The basic software components of the system are free, but the capital of these companies – and a lucrative source of income for them – is their product know-how. The popular content management system Typo3, for example, is just as good as commercial software costing €1,000, but Typo3 is freeware. But tailoring such a system to your specific application requires considerable experience, and the Typo3 developers are ready and waiting to sell you their support services.

Charging for time: the lawyer hotline

Here is another innovative price model: charge a low basic rate and bill customers for units of time. The real-life example: the popular 'lawyer hotlines' which have been set up in Germany to answer questions on traffic law, tenancy law, industrial, family or inheritance law via the telephone. The customer is charged according to the length of the telephone call, and the rate is €1.90 per minute. Customers are charged by their service provider and pay via their normal telephone bill.

Figure 4.2 The Linux Tux penguin – Microsoft's formidable rival
Source: www.linux.org

Paying lawyers for their services by the minute is far from the tradi-tional self-image of the sector. The established price model is to charge fees based on the standard rates and the amount in dispute. But you only have to look at the United States to see that there are other ways. Lawyers there are often paid for their outlay, or success premiums are agreed upon (for example when clients are claiming for damages or injuries caused).

Hire out your capital goods: rent a cow

There are even more innovative price models to be discovered. How about hiring out your capital goods instead of selling the product by the piece or the litre? Look at Switzerland and other countries to see how. For a leasing fee of 380 Swiss francs, you can be a farmer for a summer on the Tschingisfeld alm. Not personally, because of course the cow you lease will be given the best professional care. You can even go and take a look at 'your' cow. And at the end of the summer, you receive the 'yield' from your cow in the form of premium-quality Alpine cheese, which you can enjoy yourself, give away as presents or sell.

Depending on how much milk the cow gives, there are additional costs, for example 0.40 Swiss francs per litre milking charge and a maximum of 0.75 Swiss francs for the cheese making. It's a very popular business idea. The farmers can pre-finance their husbandry costs, and customers look forward to receiving their top-quality cheese made with milk from their very own cow.

More and more farmers are introducing this system. For example, you can lease a hen for a constant supply of fresh eggs, or lease a pig and look forward to tasty ham. It's even possible to lease your own vegetable plot, but you have to work it and harvest it yourself, though the farmer will sow and tend it until spring. More and more farmers are jumping on this bandwagon. It won't make you a millionaire or revolutionize the world, but it's a welcome source of additional income for farmers.

Pre-financed by the consumer: Einstürzende Neubauten

One enterprise whose 'staff' really deserve the name 'business unconventionalists' is industrial Sturm-und-Drang rock band Einstürzende Neubauten. The band actually managed to get their fans to pre-finance their next project, as the band itself lacked the capital.

You will now be seeing in your mind's eye a rock group dressed in suits and ties, drawing up business plans and then traipsing from one potential investor to the next. But that didn't quite suit the image of Einstürzende Neubauten, and so they came up with another way to finance their next album. For a charge of €35, fans could follow the recording sessions via livestream over the internet and comment on them in the chat room. They could also purchase a Neubauten e-mail address (such as suzi@neubauten.org), listen to new songs and – the most important thing of all – they received recordings on CD and DVD that were not available in the stores.

This unusual idea was the brainchild of Erin Zhu, Californian webmaster of www.neubauten.org, who spent many years working for internet companies in Silicon Valley. The project was necessary because the band's financial situation wasn't particularly rosy, as Blixa Bargeld, head of the Berlin group, freely admits: 'We are a band with a world-wide reputation, but we don't rake in astronomical sums.' The idea worked. Three webcams were installed in the band's Berlin recording studios and transmitted the pictures to the internet. Altogether, almost 2,000 'music producers' paid €35 each to finance the project.

You might not find it so surprising that a rock band has to find an innovative way to finance its next CD, but would you have thought that religious orders might need to look for new sources of income – and that you would find business unconventionalists there?

Materializing the immaterial: rent-a-nun

'Adopt a Sister' is the name of a programme set up by the Sisters of St Francis of the Third Order Regular of Williamsville, New York. Anyone who wants to do a good deed and at the same time get some support from 'above' can participate. The programme is quite serious and offers attractive rates.

You can 'adopt' a nun for one, two or five years in return for a donation of between US$100–500. In return, you have the best wishes and prayers of the Reverend Sister.

Innovative price models as an alternative to subsidies

In these days when every announcement that governments are cutting subsidies and other state aid is greeted with immediate calls for 'compensatory' support measures, this is a very encouraging example. It shows that there is a better way than relying on support from the state. Instead, this institution – which probably has its problems with the subject of innovation – came up with a very smart and innovative idea.

In fact, all these examples show that with the help of creativity, inventiveness and a generous dose of courage, you can find alternative paths. That's wonderful reading even for the most fervent defenders of the status quo, whose reaction to any change is to call for solutions from politicians and the dispensing of subsidies. It makes no sense to keep

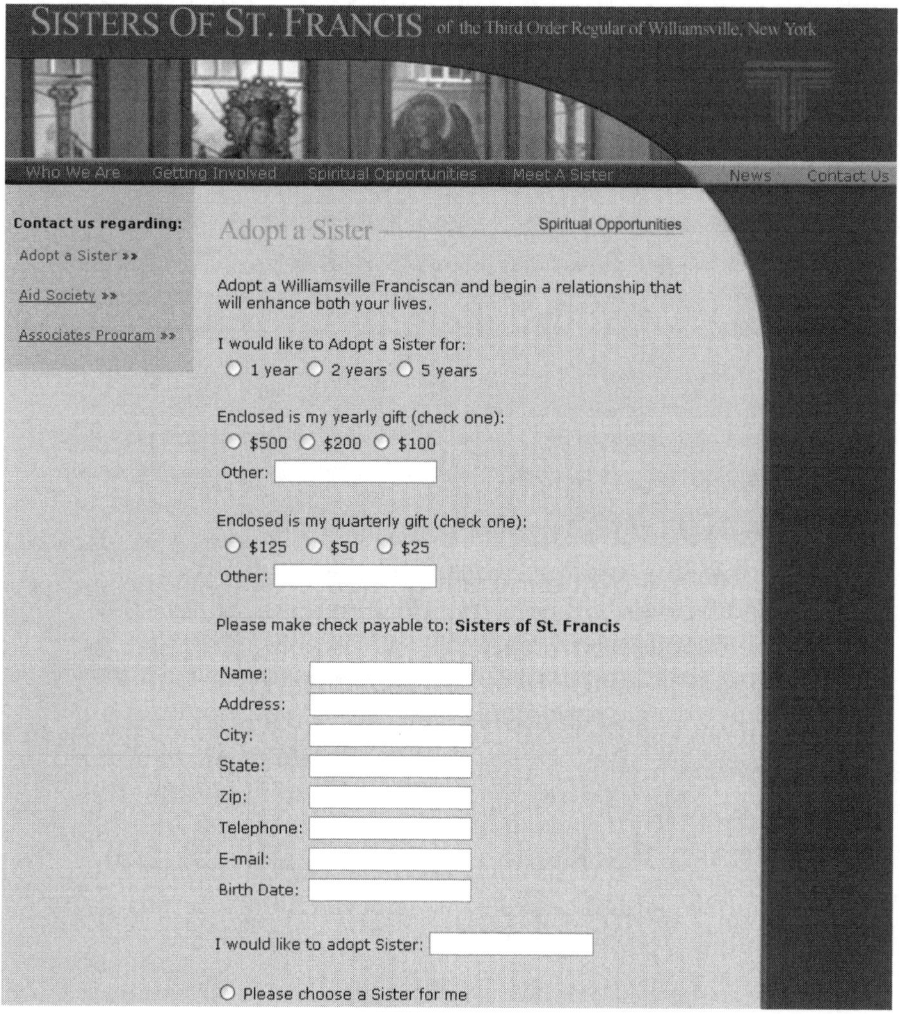

Figure 4.3 Rent a nun – and get a little help from above
Source: Sisters of St Francis of Williamsville, www.wmsvlfranciscans.org

shoring up outdated business models and industries. Society pays too high a price in the end!

As Gary Hamel so aptly put it, 'The goal is not to embalm dinosaurs through subsidies, protectionism and preferential procurement policies.' Instead, we must try to recognize change in advance and be flexible and inventive enough to take appropriate action.

What all these examples also show is how it is possible to cast aside established financing models by means of business unconventionality.

And the new price model will be doubly effective. It helps to improve your returns, but above all it helps you to differentiate yourself from the rest of the field. Suddenly, people are talking about you. This is a factor which cannot be emphasized strongly enough. If you introduce a really innovative price model, the marketing effect can be enormous!

Business unconventionality box

Keen observers of human nature have always known that it is easier to sell people something expensive than something cheap.

William Somerset Maugham, English author and dramatist

Don't waste your energy trying to optimize the established price model for your industry or trying to be just that little bit cheaper than your competitors. Create your own price model! Be inventive, courageous and creative, and turn the established price models for your industry upside down. It's not about being cheaper than your competitors, but smarter. Remember the lawyer hotline which charges not according to standard rates or the amount in dispute but in telephone call units, or Lauda Motion, which hires out Smarts for the amazing price of just €1 a day – a clever and unconventional idea: Find a third party to bear the costs.

Price polarization: send your prices skyrocketing or plummeting – and win

Price is the preferred method of elbowing your competitors off the market. It seems to be an unwritten rule. But what can you do? Do you have to stand ready to parry every blow that a rival company aims at you? The answer, in a word, is *no*. The solution: move the playing field. Don't waste time racking your brains over how to be just a few cents cheaper than your competitors. Instead, concentrate on getting yourself a true competitive edge, as the low-price airlines did. They didn't focus on being 2 or 3 per cent cheaper than the established airlines. They asked themselves, how can we make our tickets 60 or 70 per cent cheaper? And of course, you can turn the question around and ask, how can we get customers to pay not just 2 or 3 per cent but 30 or even 50 per cent more for our products or services? You will only find the answers to these questions if you dare to be different.

Achieve more: taking price models apart

Take Irish low-price airline Ryanair. Customers book online, so the company doesn't have to pay commission to travel agents. Ryanair drastically reduces take-off and landing charges by avoiding the big expensive airports and flying to smaller provincial ones. It aims for full capacity utilization of its planes, reduces ground time to a minimum, and so on. This unconventional strategy enables Ryanair to keep flying costs per mile far lower than, for example, Lufthansa ever could. And by cutting costs to a minimum, they can sell their tickets at such unbeatable prices.

The concept behind this is interesting. The customer only pays for the bare essentials, there are no frills. Companies are forced to take their value creation chains apart (deconstruction) and ask themselves, where are we creating value for the customer?

What is the customer prepared to pay for? Boost your market share by refusing to accept conventional price limits.

Rule 13 of business unconventionality

Price polarization: send your prices skyrocketing or plummeting – and win.

Conventional thinking: you try to find ways to charge your customers a few per cent more than your competitors or to offer your products or services a few per cent cheaper than the others.
Business unconventionality: you refuse to accept that there are price limits in your industry, either maximum or minimum prices. Find ways to charge 50 or 100 per cent more – or less – than your competitors.

Drastically increase or reduce your prices – and make sure your customers know why. Discount bakeries and cheap hairdressing salons on the one hand, hand-selected coffee beans and first-class service on the other: Whatever pleases your customers!

Transcend the value creation chain: a sample calculation

If your aim is to get a competitive edge by offering the lowest prices as Ryanair did, then you are going to have to take the value creation chains apart. Offer customers only what they are willing to pay for. No gimmicks, or no frills as the airlines say. The magic word is deconstruction, which is achieved by cutting out certain customary services and deliberately questioning organizational principles:

- Simple departure point/destination model: the airline flies passengers from A to B.
- Use of secondary airports: Ryanair uses few big airports as these are usually expensive and overcrowded. And as Europe is densely populated, you can reach more people by flying to smaller airports.
- Less service: no free drinks or newspapers on board, which represents a saving of 6 per cent.
- Longer flying time: Ryanair pilots fly 800 hours a year compared with the European average of 450 to 550 hours. Planes are ready for take-off just 30 minutes after landing – the average in the industry is one hour.
- Cost reduction through online booking: 96 per cent of Ryanair tickets are bought online, so Ryanair doesn't need a network of travel agencies. Thus Ryanair can enter new markets more easily – it doesn't take long to translate a website into the language of the country in question.
- More seats: seats are installed closer together, allowing Ryanair to install up to three dozen more seats per plane, meaning a bonus of 16 per cent.
- Simpler processes: on Ryanair flights, passengers have free choice of seats, doing away with the need for complicated tickets and boarding cards.
- No frequent traveller programmes or lounges: together with the simplification of processes, this brings savings of 10 per cent.
- Direct marketing: Ryanair sells its own tickets via the internet, cutting out intermediaries and saving 10 per cent.
- More efficient management: fewer and highly motivated staff sharing in success by employee participation schemes. Less rigidly defined areas of responsibility
- On-ground services provided by external companies, bringing savings of up to 6 per cent.
- Skilful purchasing of new aircraft: by purchasing larger planes, Ryanair has continually boosted its capacity. It also took advantage of the lull in the market after 9/11 and bought about 150 Boeing 737s for between US$25–30 million each (the standard price is US$62 million).

Ryanair is the prototype of successful deconstruction. And you can learn a lot from it! Ask yourself, what are the established price models in my industry? Does the customer really want all the features we consider 'standard'? Or can we put together an interesting new offering by deliberately cutting out certain components?

Ask your customers: or Aldi

How can you find out which elements of your offering your customers would be willing to do without? A simple but effective solution would be to leave your office and go out and ask your customers. The simplest way to evaluate your company's offering and to find out which elements may be unnecessary or could be offered for an additional charge is to walk a mile in your customer's shoes and buy your own products. Only by standing in front of the shelves in the store or talking to the sales personnel yourself will you notice the important details.

Another way to collect ideas is to take a look at companies that have already established a long tradition of deconstruction: the discounters. They know exactly where their core competence lies. Their strategy is limited to just a few activities. And they are also unequivocal about what they won't do. This is an important element for successful strategy, but one that is often neglected. The best example of how effective it is to define what your company does not do is Aldi, which keeps a list of activities it will not engage in. All goods are sold out of the box and are delivered on pallets. All goods are positioned in the store according to logistic considerations and to facilitate the work of Aldi's employees and thus increase productivity. Few statistics are kept, and the company deliberately refrains from the regular gathering and accumulation of all kinds of data. There are no complicated purchasing regulations, and everyone has clearly defined goals and areas of responsibility that are strictly adhered to.

Maximize, don't optimize: discount bakeries

The first important question you have to ask yourself when considering an innovative price model is, how can we achieve maximum benefit for the customer? The second question is, how can we ensure that this benefit fits in with the company's other goals?

The discount bakeries provide a good example of how this can be accomplished. The maximum customer benefit is high-quality, fresh bread, cakes and rolls at unbeatable prices. How can this benefit be achieved with the existing potential of the company? By carefully cutting out unnecessary steps! The goods don't have to be packed by the bakery staff and handed to the customer over the counter. Cut out all the services the price-conscious consumer doesn't need, and keep the organization lean – this is the recipe for the success of discount bakeries like BackWerk, Backhouse and Backfactory. They apply the self-service principle to bread, cakes and rolls. Customers select the products from the shelves and pay at the central cash desk. In this way, these chains can offer their goods at prices on average 30 per cent lower than those of conventional bakeries – although customers do have a more limited selection of products to choose from. The new discount bakeries are chain stores, so they save even more money by buying in bulk. And customers seem to like the concept – these newcomers to the industry are expanding.

The concept is similar to that of the low-price airlines: They gain a competitive edge with their low prices, which are possible because they employ fewer staff and offer less service. The stores are plain and sparsely decorated, the range of products available much more limited than in the traditional bakeries. Customers take a tray, which is lined with paper, use tongs to remove the products from the shelves, pay for them and pack them themselves. Only one or two people are required to bake the ready-mixed dough, already made up for baking and stored on pallets in the freezer room, and to restock the shelves as required. And there is only one cashier on duty.

These discount bakeries need no specially trained bakery sales personnel, but can employ unskilled labour. In a traditional bakery, staff account for between 35 and 50 per cent of costs; at the discount stores it is only 20 to 25 per cent. The range of products is usually limited to about 100 different items, compared with more than 300 at traditional baker's shops. The discounters purchase the deep-frozen ready-to-bake products wherever they are available at a good price. Computerized cash desks register which goods sell best. This helps the discounters to predict demand over the day, so that they only bake what they can expect to sell. More efficient planning means that some discounters have only 2 per cent leftover products at the end of the day, while conventional bakeries can expect 10 to 15 per cent. And all these advantages mean better prices for the consumers, on average one-third lower than those of traditional bakeries.

Customer benefit as a guiding principle: Formule-1 hotels

French hotel chain Accor is a good example of successful application of the principle of deconstruction. It also shows how you can proceed systematically to get a clear picture of customer benefit and which elements of your offering are necessary and which superfluous.

The story of Accor's new product line begins in the mid-1980s, when the situation for one- and two-star hotels in France was grim. They had fewer and fewer guests but high fixed costs that they could only hope to cover if their hotels operated at full capacity. In such an extreme situation, where companies are under great pressure to come up with a solution and do it fast, lukewarm, overcautious or copycat strategies will at best just about enable you to survive and at worst be your ruin. Accor realized this and adopted a new strategy. It asked itself, which components of our offering are really important for customers spending the night in a one- or two-star hotel?

To find the answers, Accor interviewed its guests and asked them what they were looking for in a hotel of that category. On the basis of the information it received, it developed a new concept, the Formule-1 hotels, offering good beds, cleanliness and a quiet atmosphere far beyond the standards for a two-star hotel, but at the price of a one-star establishment.

Accor's costs per hotel room are far lower than those of the average one-star hotel. Formule-1 hotels don't have restaurants or lounges, and the room furnishings, size and additional services are trimmed to the minimum. In other words, Accor deliberately cut the frills, stripping away all elements its customers were not prepared to pay for (deconstruction).

Rational – fast – cheap: the impossible hairdresser

In all areas of life, consumers are accustomed to being lured with special offers, advertising and attractive packaging. The hairdressing business is no exception. There are customer loyalty cards which entitle you to a free haircut after a certain number of visits, while other salons offer additional services such as free cosmetics tips, a glass of prosecco or free conditioning mousse. If you want to survive in such a tough environment – and this is probably not only true of the hairdressing business – you have to be unique and achieve differentiation in order to stand out from the rest. Japanese hairdressing chain QBNet has achieved differentiation via the lowest price. QBNet has 200 salons in Japan – and undercuts the average price by an amazing 66 per cent.

What is the recipe? At QBNet there is no receptionist, and customers pay at a machine, which issues them with a ticket. They take a seat in the next available chair and present this ticket to the hairdresser, who only cuts hair, but no longer washes or dries it. That is done by the Air-Wash-Head-Vacuum-System, which is suspended from the ceiling much like a salon hairdryer.

A sensor in each chair registers whether the chair is occupied, and prospective customers can see from the 'traffic lights' at the door how full the salon is. Green means they won't have to wait, yellow that the waiting time is at most five minutes, and red indicates longer waiting times. The capacity utilization data is forwarded to company headquarters. Salons operating according to this model are very popular in large cities, and their customers are people who are price-conscious, in a hurry or people who simply appreciate quick and uncomplicated service.

Differentiation through high prices

Of course, you can't help but be impressed by the companies who succeed in establishing a clear profile on the market by means of high prices, although high prices do not necessarily mean high sales costs. There may be a great difference between what you charge for and what the customers think they are paying for, because the company's price structure and the customers' value structures are not always identical. When you buy a comb in a chemist's shop, you are paying for well-groomed hair; when you buy a newspaper you are paying for information or entertainment.

> Outstanding companies compete on value and not on price alone. One of the biggest mistakes managers make is assuming that value and price mean the same thing to customers. They do not. Price is part of value, but it is not equivalent.
>
> Leonard L Berry, marketing professor at Texas A & M University

Companies that understand their customers' value structures can become innovators in price. There are examples from many different industries, for example the Canadian Cirque du Soleil, which gave the circus a whole new alignment and was thus able to redefine the price structures. Tickets for the Cirque du Soleil cost between twice and three times as much as for Circus Krone, Europe's biggest circus. Or think of Vertu, a subsidiary of Nokia, which specializes in the production of luxury mobile phones for a VIP clientele. While the average mobile phone buyer would expect to get the phone more or less for free when signing a contract with a provider, customers spend the equivalent of the price of a nice holiday on a Vertu mobile. Vertu phones are not only elegant in design, but give customers round-the-clock access to a concierge, who will, for example, make hotel, restaurant or theatre bookings for them. Or think of the examples we mentioned in the section on product design: Method, Bang & Olufsen, Kartell, Alessi and many others have realized that an attractive and pleasing design can also send your prices skyrocketing.

> The more customers perceive the product as a 'lucky opportunity' or a real 'bargain', the less they will quibble at the price.
>
> Heinz Goldmann, business consultant

Give your product an image makeover: luxury potato chips

Potato chips? A mass-produced product where only the price counts? Not always. Kettle has successfully managed to dodge this pressure point and redefined its chips as a high-price luxury product. Kettle chips are hand-cooked using special potato varieties and fried in the finest sunflower oil. Kettle's USP is superior flavour and natural ingredients. And satisfied customers spread the word, so Kettle does not engage in conventional advertising. Originally, the company made the conscious decision to avoid retail outlets, focusing instead on bars, restaurants and delicatessens as 'premium' points of sale, where it was not difficult to maintain the high price of up to €4 a packet. Now Kettle chips can also be found in selected supermarkets, although the company has remained true to its concept, which was not to allow the brand to become a mass-produced article. The result is continuous positive growth in a shrinking overall market. Kettle is market leader in the premium price segment.

Figure 4.4 Kettle chips – luxury for the masses

Source: Kettle Foods Inc, www.kettlefoods.com

Kettle's rules for success:

- Make your product irresistible.
- Believe in the value of the business.
- Establish a brand that triggers emotional attachment.
- Strive to establish long-term relationships with customers.
- Always listen to what the customer has to say.
- Reply to each complaint individually.
- Remain patient and rely on word-of-mouth advertising.

And by the way, other companies in the same market segment are now trying to copy Kettle's success. In Great Britain in particular, there are more and more snack food products on the market that try to score points with their organic, health-promoting ingredients, gentle cooking methods or simply with unusual flavours, leaving the low-price region of the market behind them. After all, you do expect to pay more for luxury!

Business unconventionality box

The real discovery is not finding an unknown land, but learning to see things with different eyes.

Marcel Proust, French writer

You don't have to reinvent the price! All you have to do is question the established price models of your industry. Your task: to develop ways to charge 50 or even 100 per cent more – or less – for your products or services than your competitors.

Think of Ryanair, which became hugely successful by reducing its service to those elements customers are really willing to pay for, or Japan's QBNet hairdressing chain, which took a close look at its value creation chain, cut all the frills and deliberately questioned established industry principles. The result: a unique market presence and clear differentiation.

Pricing in-between. Be smart – position yourself in the middle of the market

Companies that focus on the same target groups and follow the same price strategy as the rest of the field are finding themselves in a tough competitive environment. Why? To understand this, just think back to your first lecture on the basics of business administration, and the idea of the 'perfect competitive environment' where every company in the industry follows the same strategy and has similar resources at its disposal. The result: everyone makes just enough profit to survive. And that is exactly where the problem lies, because such an environment produces companies that imitate each other's price strategies right down to the smallest detail.

Think carefully before you imitate: look what happened to Lufthansa!

In many industries, companies tend to adopt similar strategies because it is logical that any concept promising success or that has already proved successful will be imitated. Of course, imitation is not a bad thing, as long as you have your own strategy for other business areas. However, all too often companies imitate every detail that has made others successful without stopping to consider that their own starting point is a different one and that the model may not be a 100 per cent fit for their company.

Let us return to the example of the airlines here. When low-price airlines conquered larger and larger shares of the market and started to poach corporate clients, too, the old-established airlines began to get nervous. And so for some time, Lufthansa experimented with a programme of increased efficiency to try to elbow out these intruders by trying to outdo them in cutting services to a bare minimum: no frills, less space between the seats and cuts in the already spartan in-flight service.

> When people no longer believe in your product, it's a death sentence for your company.
>
> Sir Bob Geldof, musician and founder of Live Aid

Bad move! By trying to beat the cut-price operators at their own game and imitating their cost structures, Lufthansa risks damaging its reputation as a premium service provider. And above all, it risks angering an important target group: the so-called 'Senators', top customers who clock up more than 150,000 miles a year in the Lufthansa frequent-flyer programme Miles & More. There are two reasons that this strategy is dangerous. First, because Lufthansa has higher operating costs than the low-price airlines, it needs higher prices – and it can only justify these by providing a noticeably better service. And second, the image of a low-price operator on short-haul flights contradicts the established image of Lufthansa as a provider of high-level service on long-haul flights, a picture the company is striving to maintain by investing several hundred million euros in luxury lounges and beds in business class. And the really damaging effect is that following this path means that a company loses its credibility with its own customers.

What can we learn from this? Don't try to be all things to all people. You can't be a premium company and at the same time offer your premium customers the same service as a cut-price operator. You can be successful at either end of the spectrum, but not at both. You can't be a premium operator and a cut-price operator at the same time and for one and the same target group.

Another interesting possibility is to find a new strategic price group.

Rule 14 of business unconventionality:

Pricing in-between. Be smart – position yourself in the middle of the market.

Conventional thinking: you focus on optimizing your position within an existing price group.

Business unconventionality: you refuse to accept the established price groups for your industry. Instead, you recombine the special features of existing price groups to achieve better customer orientation and create your own strategic price group.

To illustrate how to set about creating a new strategic price group, let's take a look at the hotel and restaurant trade. Just imagine that you're on your lunch break and are looking for a snack that's light and healthy, but still quick. You could go to a conventional restaurant, but the service there takes time in the lunch hour. You're not the only one trying to grab a bite to eat in their lunch break. And eating in restaurants every lunch hour can be a bit hard on the wallet, too.

Upgrading traditional business models: soup bars and sandwich chains

There are several alternatives. What about popping in to McDonald's, Burger King or Pizza Hut or visiting the nearest hamburger stand? Quick, cheap, but not very healthy in the long term – as was demonstrated by Morgan Spurlock's film *Supersize Me*, in which the director lived on McDonald's food for 30 days and gained 25 pounds in the process.

The situation just cries out for someone to invent a new business model providing healthy fast food at a price somewhere between the hamburger stand and a restaurant. And there you have your opportunity! Today, you will find a restaurant of the 'new soup bar' type in every large city anywhere in the world. These soup bars serve tasty, healthy soups and stews to suit every appetite. The idea originally came from New York – where else? Al's Soup Kitchen International was the first of the new 'soup bars'. And because it has very clear ideas on how it expects its customers to behave – stand in line, know what you want and have your money ready, then wait on the left for your order – and as a result of the deliberately unfriendly tone in which they are informed of this, Al's Soup Kitchen achieved notoriety in the television series *Seinfeld* as 'Soup Nazi'. If you would like to see it for yourself, you will find it at 259A West 55th Street, between 7th and 8th Street in New York. Stand in line and hear how Al treats his customers. But you don't necessarily have to go to New York. There are now soup bars in London, Berlin, Nuremberg, Dresden, Hamburg, Munich, Cologne and so on.

Want another example? Sandwich chain Cosi has successfully positioned itself between the lower strategic price group, the fast food chains, and the upper price group, the conventional restaurants. It is rapidly becoming the Starbucks of the sandwich world. Cosi's recipe is the same as the one that made Starbucks so successful: high quality, a convivial atmosphere and food as an experience. Instead of wolfing down their 99-cent burgers at greasy tables, Cosi's guests can enjoy the scent of fresh-baked bread, subtle jazz music playing in the background and an extremely pleasant atmosphere. Customers don't even mind that a sandwich costs US$7 and more.

Cosi's success proves that the concept is right. Although there are at least 10 cheaper places to get lunch within a radius of 50 metres, 'No one has bread like Cosi', the customers explain.

Be clever – be different

Creating your own strategic price group is a good idea, and for two reasons. First, it means that you will not be competing directly with all the other companies on the market, because you will be creating your own price category. And second, it will force you to think long and hard about ways to differentiate yourself from the rest of the field.

Where will you find ideas on how to differentiate yourself? Even though we believe that it is a good idea to get input from external sources, let us add one word of warning here. There is an ever-growing army of eager-beaver consultants all ready to advise you in this area. But it's a good idea to be sceptical when a big consulting firm claims 'We know your industry inside out.' Why? Because what it really means is, 'We have already worked for 20 other companies in the industry, so we are in the ideal position to recommend exactly the same best practices to you.' This would of course mean that all companies would follow a similar strategy and would not achieve differentiation at all! So, sometimes you just have to rely on your own ideas.

That's what Werner Kieser did when he was considering how he could differentiate by offering a unique gym concept and creating his own strategic price group. So Kieser took a pinch of deconstruction – taking apart the company's value creation chain and pinpointing which elements create added value for the customer – and hey presto, he had the concept of Kieser Training.

Inexpensive, but not cheap: Kieser Training

Within just a few years, Kieser Training became the largest provider of health-oriented fitness training in the German-speaking area. In clear contrast to the other companies on the market, Kieser follows a principle of reduction to the essentials. Minimalist interiors for the training rooms, no bar selling protein drinks, no music, no television, no aerobics or yoga classes. And no sauna, whirlpool or massages either! Instead, Kieser specializes in preventative and therapeutic weight training to promote health and boost performance.

Figure 4.5 Kieser Training – the alternative to the 'sweatshop'
Source: Kieser Training AG

You don't go there to have fun or to sculpt the perfect body. You go there to take care of your body, your muscles and musculoskeletal system. As this is a highly specialized service, the philosophy of the Kieser fitness programme only appeals to specific target groups. The most important customer group is middle-aged and elderly people, well educated and from a middle-class background. And 80 per cent of Kieser's clients had never been to a gym before.

Kieser's prices are based on the principle that 'Kieser Training is affordable for everyone', in order to attract as broad a target group as possible and to ensure a clear and easily understandable price policy. In other words, Kieser aims to be inexpensive – but not cheap. Kieser offers as few special rates as possible, and the prices are significantly cheaper that the membership fees charged by the lifestyle-oriented fitness temples.

Staying different: differentiation starts at the top!

Executives who spend a great deal of their time studying the same magazines, attending the same trade fairs and listening to the same guest speakers at conferences and seminars only accelerate the speed with which their strategies and actions come to mimic those of their competitors. If there is no room for fresh ideas and an objective view of your own industry, the inevitable will happen. Strategies will become increasingly similar, new products and services are imitated the moment they appear on the market, and people within these organizations begin not only to dress and sound alike, they even start to think alike.

Don't get us wrong: we have nothing whatsoever against the big banks. But seriously, if we had crept out last night while everyone was asleep, picked 50 top managers from the four big German banks and swapped them around so that they were all working for one of their competitors, do you really think the customers would have noticed?

Inexpensive, but service-oriented: JetBlue

Business unconventionalists have realized that the only way to escape is to achieve clear differentiation. Customers should know whether they are doing business with Bank A or Bank B – and they should know whether they are flying with airline X or airline Y. And you can take our word for it: you know whether you're flying JetBlue or Ryanair. Both airlines offer flights at prices considerably lower than those of the big airlines, but JetBlue has created its own distinctive strategic price group. JetBlue does not see itself as a low-price operator, but as a new airline with high ideals. JetBlue lays great emphasis on passenger comfort, a very positive service experience and word-of-mouth advertising.

JetBlue's concept differs considerably from that of the typical low-price airline. Prices are around 40 per cent cheaper than those of the large US airlines. JetBlue sees itself not as an airline, but as a service enterprise.

'Customers must have a good experience with your product at every single point of contact,' says JetBlue President David Neeleman. That means brand-new aircraft, leather seats, plenty of legroom and free satellite TV with 24 channels at every seat. Efficient processes ensure that JetBlue's service is seen as exemplary. And while others find air travel without tickets the height of modernity, at JetBlue, even the administration, pilots and mechanics all work without paper.

Business unconventionality box

To predict the future, you don't necessarily need to be clairvoyant. But you do have to be unconventional.

Your price strategy, too, needs to be unconventional. Refuse to accept the established price models for your industry. Instead, recombine the special features of existing price models to achieve optimum customer orientation and create your own strategic price model. Remember sandwich chain Cosi, which has cleverly positioned itself between the cheap fast food chains and expensive restaurants. US airline JetBlue employs a similar concept. It is not quite as cheap as no-frills airlines like Ryanair, but still offers flights at prices considerably lower than those of American Airlines or Delta. And the best thing about JetBlue is that it offers above-average service, seating, entertainment and legroom.

The Rockefeller Principle: give away the lamp and sell the oil

'Give away the lamp and sell the oil', was the motto of oil magnate John D Rockefeller, and that was in the mid-19th century! It was obvious – if you had a lamp, you wanted to use it, and to do so, you needed petroleum. And of course Mr Rockefeller supplied the petroleum, but at a price!

Many companies overlook the fact that they can earn much more with follow-up orders, maintenance and servicing, spare parts, materials, accessories and so on than with the product itself.

Rule 15 of business unconventionality

The Rockefeller Principle: give away the lamp and sell the oil.

Conventional thinking: you calculate your services individually, focusing on profit from the direct sale of products.
Business unconventionality: you offer your customers low initial prices and earn your money with the customers' operating costs.

Don't get us wrong. The purpose of this section is not to teach you how to 'rip your customers off'. That would be a very unwise strategy, because customers, like elephants, never forget. They notice when they are being treated badly and will make sure that all their friends and acquaintances get to hear about it. As so often, the art lies in finding the golden middle, offering customers low initial prices and earning money with their running costs.

The printer manufacturers have done just that. Inkjet printers are inexpensive, but the ink in the special cartridges is fast becoming one of the most expensive liquids in the world. The Rockefeller Principle!

Another typical example: You can get a mobile phone contract complete with phone for nothing – but the charges for phone calls, SMS, MMS and services are high.

The principle is always the same: Manufacturers make no profit on the initial sale. Instead, their objective is to make a profit over the entire product life cycle. The product costs next to nothing or is free, while turnover and profit are generated by subsequent costs or the sale of materials. This approach can be seen in many markets. AOL, for example, subsidizes the sale of personal computers and peripheral equipment if customers sign a 24-month contract binding them to AOL. Electrical equipment needs expensive batteries, and yes, your new highlighter is rechargeable, but – you know the rest!

The Rockefeller Principle and the pleasures of drinking espresso

For a long time, producing coffee machines was not a particularly exciting business. Consumers bought their coffee machine for €30, and that was the end of the story for the manufacturers, because the consumers then bought their ground coffee in packets from the supermarket. New offerings according to the principle 'Give away the lamp and sell the oil' create significantly higher opportunities. Manufacturers have developed new coffee machines that only take special coffee pads developed by the manufacturer. If you buy such a machine, you pay an average of five times more for your coffee than when you use the traditional filter coffee machines.

Nespresso from Nestlé comes in packs containing just the right amount of coffee for one cup of high-quality espresso, but the customer first has to buy the machine that processes these packs. The manufacturer promises customers convenience in combination with premium-quality coffee – and they love it. The interesting thing about this model is that it offers convenience for the customer and high profit per cup of coffee for the manufacturer.

The Philips Senseo machine also brews high-quality coffee to match that produced by any €500 machine. The Senseo machine costs only €59 and has a very attractive design. Philips and its partners, coffee producers Douwe Egberts, make their money on the sale of the coffee, because only Senseo pads fit Senseo machines. To be fair, we should perhaps mention that for some time now, we have been making our coffee in a Senseo machine – and it tastes wonderful.

Earning good money with spare parts: get a Gillette shave

If users of electric shavers need a new shaver foil or a new cutter block, they can't just go out and buy any old cheap no-name product. The shavers are designed so that only spare parts produced by the original manufacturer will fit, and guess what? These spare parts are quite expensive. And if it works with electric shavers, then it ought to work with wet razors, too. That was Gillette's idea when it entered the market, offering cheap razors that could only be fitted with Gillette razor blades. The real money is made from the sale of the razor blades, and customers have to buy them from Gillette.

This is a very effective business model which makes regular subsequent purchases necessary. There is one danger, however: We haven't yet heard of anyone selling copies of Gillette razor blades, but there are already quite a few companies that refill printer cartridges – and they convince their customers with the argument of a lower price.

Making money from additional costs: the extras make the difference

The Rockefeller Principle can also be applied in the services sector. For example, there are cruises where the tickets are inexpensive but the operators make their money with the additional costs. Journalists from US daily *USA Today* booked a seven-day Caribbean cruise at the bargain price of US$269 for two, and enjoyed the good life while they were on board. When the ship returned to its port of departure at the end of the cruise, they were presented with a bill for the proud sum of US$1,367.67. It seems the days when a cruise was an all-inclusive package deal are over.

Business unconventionality box

When John D Rockefeller was hoping to sell oil to the Chinese at the end of the 19th century, he showed his more generous side. He bought tons of oil lamps, shipped them to Asia and gave them away in China. They were so pleased that of course they then bought the fuel for their lamps from the clever oil trader. Rockefeller thus secured an enormous market because he realized that first you have to create demand.

You too can apply this principle. Offer your customers low initial prices and earn your money with the operating costs. This is not an invitation to rip your customers off, but an unconventional approach that can work for you, if you set about it in the right way. Nestlé shows you how. The customer buys a Nespresso machine at a relatively low price, and Nestlé earns its money with the sale of the corresponding pre-portioned packs containing just the right amount of coffee for one cup of espresso.

Or think of the cruise travel market, where some operators are applying the good old Rockefeller Principle. The tickets are cheap, and they earn their money on the additional costs.

Personalized price: let the customer set the price

We have already examined a whole range of possibilities for applying the principles of business unconventionality to the question of pricing:

- You can charge the customer directly or have a third party pay.
- You can bundle various components or charge individually for them.
- You can charge a low basic price and earn your money with follow-up sales.
- You can work with fixed charges.

Or you can let customers set the price. How can customers set the price? The price can depend on how urgently they need the goods or services, what additional services they require or the degree of individualization necessary. You see, there is a whole variety of ways in which you can achieve differentiation here and also create a benefit both for your customers and for you!

Rule 16 of business unconventionality

Personalized price: let the customer set the price.

Conventional thinking: you charge fixed prices for your products and services, irrespective of the demand and what customers are prepared to pay.
Business unconventionality: you set up a price system based on demand and what the customer is willing to pay.

The example of the cut-price airlines shows that it isn't always easy to find the right – demand-oriented – price model. If you have a few seats still available, should you sell them at a lower last-minute price? Or should you charge more because business travellers often book flights at short notice and the price doesn't matter to them?

Demand dictates the price: behind the scenes at Air Berlin

Let's take a look at how Air Berlin has solved this problem. The magazine *McKinleyWissen* analysed the pricing systems of the cut-price airlines using Air Berlin as an example. The system is quite simple and consists of the following two basic stages. First, only the first 20 people to book get their tickets for the advertised minimum price of, for example, €29. After that, the price rises by €10 with every 10 bookings.

This means that as a ticket price of €69 is required to cover the fixed costs for the flight – €12,700 for a plane with 184 seats – the airline is obviously going to make a loss on the cheaper tickets it sells, as only passengers number 70 and upwards will pay this threshold price. When the 101st passenger books a seat, the airline breaks even and has recovered the losses it made with the first 70 cut-price tickets. If the plane is fully booked, the last passenger to make a booking will pay €179 for his or her ticket, which means that Air Berlin needs an average of at least 101 passengers. The profit on the flight if the plane is fully booked is €5,100.

The British easyGroup is also very successful with demand-oriented pricing. All the group's companies, whether it be easyJet, easyBus, easyCinema or easyCar, follow a demand-oriented pricing system. The higher the number of bookings, the higher the price.

Hotels are also thinking again. Capacity utilization levels fluctuate, and they would like to fill their last available rooms, too. But while there are numerous internet platforms that help you find and book hotel rooms, there are no innovative, demand-oriented pricing models to be found.

We have already mentioned the NH Hotels Group, which recognized the potential for its hotels here and operates according to the same principle as the low-price airlines. 'The earlier you book, the lower the price' is the motto, and the hotel rooms are divided into different tariff groups. The first rooms are sold at the lowest price of €29. Once that tariff group is fully booked, the price rises step by step. In this price model, no refunds are given and alterations in bookings can only be made for a fee. For customers who want more flexibility, there is a flexi-tariff where bookings can be cancelled and alterations made free of charge – but the prices are higher.

Satisfied customers pay more: Hotel Tannenhof

Wagner's Hotel Tannenhof applies a different strategy. It is at present the only hotel in Germany with a recommended price for the first three days of your stay. Satisfied customers pay the recommended price.

Should customers be dissatisfied, for whatever reason, they decide how much they pay for the first three nights.

And another innovative offer for hotel guests: really smart travellers can negotiate the price of a night in a hotel with one of the numerous 'name your price' companies operating via the internet. The principle is simple. The hotel guest goes online and enters the price he or she is prepared to pay for a night in a four- or five-star hotel; the agent (such as www.priceline.com) adds its fee and offers the customer a total price. If the customer accepts the offer, they conclude a contract. The customer does not, however, know at which of the hotels in the selected category, and in the selected part of town, he or she will be staying. Famous chains such as Raffles, Marriott, Hilton and InterContinental are among those participating in the scheme.

Do your sums!

Take a close look at your company from the perspective of easyGroup. The central question is: how can we keep costs extremely low and still boost capacity utilization or demand exponentially? easyGroup masters this difficult balancing act in all its business areas (cinemas, internet cafés, cruises, airline, car hire, hotels, credit cards, pizza home delivery service, landline and contract mobile phones). So the question is, are you going to wait until easyGroup or some other bold intruder shows you how to revolutionize *your* industry? Or are you going to think hard about it now?

The prime objective in all cases is price differentiation and simultaneous maximization of profits, and the basic idea is to offer price-sensitive potential customers low-price product variations and price-insensitive customers high-price product variations. The customers themselves decide to which category they belong – and it's not only a question of how much money they have.

Select your price: design your personal computer

The example of personal computer manufacturer Dell shows how changing the established price models can give you a competitive edge. Dell produces and configures personal computers to the specifications of the individual customer, and only after receipt of the order. Build to order is the name of the principle. With regard to the price, this means that the customers themselves decide how much they want to spend on a new personal computer or notebook. This is possible by using an interactive configurator on the Dell website, which allows customers to select the exact configuration they want. A few days later the exact same configuration may cost more or less. At the push of a button, Dell can adjust the prices of the basic systems and the individual options to allow for market conditions. The company aims to keep its price 10 per cent below that of a comparable model purchased from a specialist dealer.

Whereas electronic stores only stock prefabricated configurations, Dell customers can decide for themselves exactly what they need and what price they are prepared to pay. There are further price options for premium customers: discounts when Dell has production capacity free or for customers who order early. Dell also has different prices for private customers, corporate clients, premium customers and government agencies, a complex pricing system established on the basis of information and prognoses concerning the customer's past and future requirements and the most popular configurations.

The advantage for Dell is an improved financial structure for the company. Dell customers pay before Dell has to pay its suppliers, so Dell can use the cash flow to finance other business areas instead of having to generate floating capital.

Discount or service? It's your decision at Haus der Musik

Haus der Musik, which sells musical instruments in Detmold, Germany, has created an innovative service offering. In its online shop at Musikalienhandel.de, customers can decide whether they want more service or a lower price, thus deciding what price they will pay for the instruments they purchase. When you have found the instrument you want, you can choose the favourable, inexpensive or cheap price bracket. Depending on the instrument, you can get up to 30 per cent discount. Now you can solicit an offer, which is sent via e-mail, telephone, SMS or fax, and then contact the company via a toll-free number at any time of the day or night to accept the offer or if you have any questions.

The difference between the price brackets is in the service. Customers who are looking for a bargain and for whom service is not so important select cheap and get up to 30 per cent discount. Those who want a range of services select inexpensive and get up to 25 per cent

Figure 4.6   Dell – customize your computer and select your price
Source: www.dell.com

discount. And for customers looking for service from a local dealer who would like to try out the instruments on the spot, there is the category of favourable (discounts of up to 20 per cent). The most important advantage of this system is that the company avoids head-on competition on price. The more all the products on the market come to resemble each other, the more hazardous a confrontation on price becomes. At Haus der Musik, the customer makes a personal decision, and this process of individualization means that the decision whether to buy is made not on price but on utility. The price is an additional factor, but not the all-important question – as long as it does not exceed the limits of what consumers find generally acceptable.

Different price groups for different needs: the Clubschiff model

The price of a cruise on an AIDA Clubschiff cruise liner depends on what the customer is prepared to pay. There are three price classes with clearly defined offerings and clearly differentiated prices. You can't dictate the price you want to pay, but you do have the choice between various price categories. In the winter season 2004/2005, Seetours introduced a new, attractive, triple-tiered price model for the AIDA Clubschiff line.

AIDA Premium offers the best price–performance ratio for customers who are looking for a dream holiday with all the trimmings. They have a free choice of cabin number and deck – from inside cabins to suites. They also have the option of making a provisional booking, which is valid for three days, for a specific date, without any commitment on their part, or they can have their names put on a waiting list. AIDA Premium customers enjoy discounts for early bookings, a fair price guarantee and reduced prices for children. The AIDA Premium price can be found in the catalogue, and each cruise can be booked as a package deal or from/to the harbour.

AIDA Vario is the ideal choice for anyone looking for a deal that accommodates his or her individual preferences and is still flexible with regard to cabin and furnishings. Here, the customer can specify the route, the ship and the cabin category – inside, outside or with balcony – but not the deck and the cabin number. The AIDA Vario price is subject to change in the course of the season, according to demand. Customers can obtain details of the current price for the various liners and departure dates via the internet, at www.aida.de, or by inquiring at their travel agency.

Finally, Just AIDA is perfect for first-time cruise passengers who are price-oriented and are primarily looking for the AIDA experience: The tour operator rewards flexibility with regard to ship, route and cabin with flexible prices that can be found on the internet or by consulting travel agents. Just AIDA represents a saving of up to €250 in comparison with the AIDA Premium price category. Customers can choose between cruises of various lengths, select the departure date and whether they want an inside or outside cabin. Just AIDA cruises can only be booked for two adults in a double cabin. This offer does not include flights, hotel bookings or reduced prices for children.

Thus, the tour operator can offer its guests the greatest possible degree of clarity and flexibility, with defined offerings that are adaptable to individual requirements and clearly set out in the catalogue. Customers choose the category that best suits their needs. Ideally, customers would be completely free to choose what they are prepared to pay for – see the example of eBay. And eBay proves that such a concept is by no means a disadvantage for the service provider. Items for sale on eBay are often sold for unexpectedly high sums when several potential buyers compete against each other and push the prices up.

Free selection of price as an advertising gimmick

Low-cost airline Hapag-Lloyd Express chose the principle of free selection of the price by the customer as a means of attracting free publicity. 'You decide on the price!' it announced when the summer flight timetables for 2004 were introduced. In practice, this meant that first-time customers could put their names down, online or via a call centre, for a flight on the routes Stuttgart–Bari, Cologne/Bonn–Bari, Berlin–Klagenfurt and Hamburg–Klagenfurt. The names of the lucky applicants were drawn in a lottery, and they paid the price they considered appropriate for this first flight.

This shows that companies can use such pricing models as a guerrilla-marketing tool. Other airlines have also experimented with 'lotteries', and planes are full in no time at all as consumers fall over themselves in the hunt for a real bargain.

Business unconventionality box

Let your customer set the price. The most important advantage for you: it allows you to avoid head-on competition.

Consistently tailor your prices to demand or to what the customers are willing to pay. This makes the decision to buy a question of utility and not of price. The price becomes just an additional piece of information, but is no longer the all-important criterion in the eyes of your customers.

Think of Haus der Musik in Detmold. When they buy online, customers can select a price category, depending on the degree of service they want. And what works for innovative medium-sized companies can be just as easily implemented by large corporations. Take Dell Computers, for example. Here, too, customers can decide how much they want to spend on a new computer with the help of the interactive configurator on the Dell website.

Free price: offer freebies to your customers and let others foot the bill

Why don't you just make your service to the customer free? You think we have finally gone just a little too far, that the strain of writing such a long book is finally telling? We can reassure you there. We're only a little bit crazy! We're not suggesting you should pass up the just rewards for your effort. But, looking at things from the point of view of business unconventionalists, why don't you let others foot the bill? Your customers will love you for it.

Rule 17 of business unconventionality

Free price: offer freebies to your customers and let others foot the bill.

Conventional thinking: you bill the 'buyer' for the services you render.
Business unconventionality: you make your service to the customer free of charge or provide it at a give-away or even symbolic price. Find a third party to foot the bill.

You think it's impossible? Many companies are already doing it successfully: Lauda Motion rents out cars for the symbolic price of €1 per day. The actual costs are borne by companies paying for advertising space on the rental cars. And Ryanair is planning to fly passengers free of charge.

The 'coffee trip' system

You already know one version of the (more or less) for free offerings. Day trips for only €9.90 with free products worth €29.95 thrown in, the so-called 'coffee trips'. Do they work? No, in most cases they don't, because such trips usually turn out to be promotional events for the producers of blankets that reputedly ward off rheumatism, magnetic cushions or 20-piece saucepan sets.

But there is a better way, and the trips are still amazingly cheap. Between four and five million Germans book bus shopping tours every year, and 76 per cent of them were satisfied or even extremely satisfied, as a study by GfK market research revealed. The institute interviewed 1,000 people, all of whom had gone on one of 48 such low-price tours lasting one or more days, allowing them to visit attractive destinations.

These trips were either partly financed by means of the promotional events mentioned above, or were subsidized by marketing councils for the regions visited, who are eager to entice people to shop there. In the case of bus tours, the restaurants along their route pay the coach tour operators to stop there. The trips are also subsidized by means of on-board sales and advertising.

There is a lot of money to be made here. On average, each passenger spends between €100 and €200 per day of the tour, depending on the target group and the destination. And research shows that sales companies make an annual turnover of more than €250 million with such tours alone.

Give it away to the user and let others pay for it

You have already seen elsewhere in this chapter how Ryanair and other low-price airlines are able to offer their cut-price flights by means of careful deconstruction. Ryanair's CEO, Michael O'Leary, even plans to fly passengers free of charge in future. 'I don't see why we shouldn't fly people for nothing and get someone else to pay,' says O'Leary, CEO of Europe's biggest low-price airline. Ryanair plans to make this possible by introducing similar refinancing models to those used by the coach tour operators, by finding sponsors to pay the cost of the flights, installing advertising displays on planes and getting car-rental firms to sponsor the kerosene. In Ryanair's plan, the airports would be the largest sponsors. Ryanair's argumentation is that as airports are rapidly becoming huge shopping malls, they ought to pay for the privilege of having customers brought to their door. O'Leary also sees hotels as potential sponsors.

In the business year 2003, a full 16 per cent of Ryanair's turnover of some €850 million and an even higher percentage of profits were generated by spin-off services such as on-board sales or commissions for selling hotel rooms, CDs or real-estate financing on the Ryanair website. O'Leary has plans to expand activities in this sector. In Ireland, free bus tours for tourists have long been financed in this way. 'When the coaches stop at some stores, the drivers collect a commission from the store owners for the money their passengers spend,' O'Leary says. 'And I think we airlines have to consider a new approach.'

Free is cool – and good for business

While the German national newspapers regularly increase their prices, the Swiss newspaper companies seem a little bit more (business) unconventional. In 2003, every day more than 720,000 people read the free newspaper *20 Minuten*, which now ranks second among the German-language newspaper publications in Switzerland behind the more sensationalist tabloid *Blick*. This represents an increase of 129 per cent since 2001. A look at our European neighbours reveals that free newspapers are extremely successful in big cities and that further expansion is to be expected. In Stockholm, the first free daily (*Metro*) appeared in 1995 and was soon making a profit. Today, *Metro* is the most popular daily newspaper in Sweden. The originators, now international group Metro International, then launched further newspapers in other large European cities, with the Netherlands, the Czech Republic and Hungary as the most profitable locations alongside Sweden.

Norwegian media group Schibsted controls its Europe-wide network of free daily newspapers from Zurich. Free daily newspapers have been launched in Switzerland, Germany, Spain and Italy, often despite strong local competition, while the British newspaper companies have largely managed to defend their domestic market from intrusion.

Cross-media marketing is the recipe behind the free newspapers. The core target group consists of young people, a consumer group largely neglected by the traditional daily papers, according to market research studies. The free papers establish themselves as independent advertising media, a form of direct marketing that reaches a large readership, has rapid growth rates and is aimed at a highly mobile audience.

Pioneers of free newspapers such as Rudi Hinterleitner from Graz or Alfons Gann from Salzburg have always taken care to ensure that their papers are not publications primarily created for advertisers, but also and above all for their readers. 'We print a newspaper that just happens to be free', is one of Styria manager Dietmar Zikulnig's favourite sayings.

Today the free papers really are serious rivals for the daily press – and should not be underestimated. In Germany, the traditional papers are engaged in a bitter struggle to ward off this unwelcome competition, maintaining that the free papers are violating the laws against unfair competition, as it is unethical to distribute newspapers free of charge. What they forget to mention is that for many years now, there have been regional weeklies mainly financed through advertising and which are also distributed free of charge. But then again, they are not in direct competition with the traditional dailies.

Are customers only interested in the price?

For the management of many companies, pricing is a very important subject that regularly gives rise to lively discussion. Unfortunately, it is a topic that all too often is only discussed when problems occur, when sales are crumbling or the figures for the latest quarter make immediate action necessary. Under pressure, companies often panic and make unwise decisions. The customer is usually blamed for the situation, and soon everyone knows why – the customer is only interested in the price. And this flawed picture of customer motivation means that suddenly the only question being asked is, what can we do to ensure that we can undercut our competitors' prices by x per cent – if not lastingly, then at least for a short time?

However, this way of tackling the problem is not very creative and is unlikely to produce the required effect. Why? Because that's what everyone else is doing! Like a hamster on a treadmill. So dare to be different, be smarter. Break out of that old routine and get off the treadmill.

Start by asking yourself one important question: if it's really true that customers are only interested in the price, then why is that so? Answer: because our goods and services are identical or almost identical to those of our competitors. We are not differentiated enough. The logical conclusion for the consumer is, if all products and services are the same, then why shouldn't I go for the lowest price?

Now turn the question around. How can you prevent customers making their decision solely on the basis of the lowest price? By differentiation. In the preceding chapters, we have seen that there are enough successful examples out there. This chapter has shown that you can use the price and pricing as a means of achieving clear differentiation – and becoming a business unconventionalist!

Business unconventionality box

If it's all a question of price, *you* should be the one talking about it, and not about offering suicidal discounts. That will only make you a 'me too' company. Think about creative strategies which make good business sense.

Make your service to the customer free of charge, sell at a give-away or even a symbolic price. Find a third party to foot the rest of the bill. Ryanair will soon be showing you how. The low-cost airline plans to fly passengers for free! How? By involving companies who wish to advertise, airports and hotels in the financing.

Off you go!

If you ask me what I have come to do in this world... I will reply: I am here to live my life out loud!

Émile Zola, French novelist

Be a business unconventionalist! Start now! No excuses, please! It doesn't matter whether you're the boss and have a desk big enough to land an army helicopter on, or are a simple clerk with a corner table. It doesn't matter whether you command a workforce of 8,000 or not even your dog listens to you. And it makes absolutely no difference whether you fly in the company jet or travel second class on the railways.

There are no excuses. It's up to you and you alone. Have the courage to make a start! Have the courage to question the status quo, existing markets, products and strategies. Experiment, think unconventionally! Stand up and be counted!

Unconventional thinking can also help you to breathe life and colour into the dull monotony of business life. Our business world today is far too grey and humourless already. It's full of grey, unexciting people who have never taken a risk but have spent their whole lives following the same old routines, while stubbornly expecting to get different results.

Barry Gibbons, former head of fast food chain Burger King, sums it all up: 'Risk taking is surgically removed before anybody is promoted to middle management, and humour is about as popular as smoking.'

The people we have described in this book are anything but grey and dull. They enjoy their work and – perhaps for that very reason – they are successful. And that's what you should be aiming for. Forget boredom and mediocrity. They're no fun and they get you nowhere.

People don't get to be successful with boring, mediocre ideas. They never have done and never will do. No way!

Play around with the unconventional strategies we offer, experiment with them. See the ideas as pieces of a puzzle that you can assemble to create an endless variety of new ideas. Find out how the individual pieces work, try to adapt the ideas to fit the situation in your own organization, mix and match them or invent new ones.

The rules of business unconventionality contained in this book are not irrefutable truths. They are tools enabling you to inject a dose of innovation and enthusiasm into established products, processes and mindsets. Learn to look over the rim of your teacup, to view old problems from new perspectives and shape your destiny.

Become a business unconventionalist. Live your life out loud! And start NOW!

Good luck!

Anja Förster and Peter Kreuz

Dream as if you'll live forever;
live as if you'll die tomorrow

James Dean

References and further reading

Bosshart, David (2007) *Cheap: How chasing discounts is changing our economies and our society*, Kogan Page, London

Foster, Richard N (1988) *The Attackers Advantage*, Simon & Schuster, London

Gibbons, Barry (1996) *This Indecision is Final. 32 management secrets of Albert Einstein, Billie Holiday, and a bunch of other people who never worked 9 to 5*, Irwin Professional, Chicago, IL

Gibbons, Barry (2001) *Dream Merchants and HowBoys: Mavericks, nutters and the road to business success*, Wiley-Vch, Weinheim, Germany

Hamel, Gary (2000) *Leading the Revolution*, Harvard Business School Press, Boston, Mass

Hamel, Gary and Prahalad, C K (1994) *Competing for the Future*, McGraw-Hill Professional, New York

Kawasaki, Guy (1995) *How to Drive Your Competition Crazy: Creating disruption for fun and profit*, Hyperion, New York

Kelly, Kevin (1998) *New Rules for the New Economy: 10 radical strategies for a connected world*, Viking, New York

Levitt, Theodore (1998) *Thinking about Management*, Free Press, New York

McKenna, Regis (2001) *Real Time Marketing*, Midas Management, Zurich, Switzerland

McKenna, Regis (2002) *Access-Marketing*, Wiley-Vch, Weinheim, Germany

Mikunda, Christian (2004) *Brand Lands, Hot Spots and Cool Spaces: Welcome to the third place and the total marketing experience*, Kogan Page, London

Ogilvy, David (2004) *Confessions of an Advertising Man*, Southbank Publishing, Manchester

Peters, Tom (1999) *Circle of Innovation: You can't shrink your way to greatness*, Vintage, New York

Peters, Tom (2004) *Re-imagine!* Dorling Kindersley, London

Pine, Joseph and Gilmore, James (1999) *Experience Economy: Work is theatre and every business a stage*, Harvard Business School Press, Boston, MA

Prahalad, C K and Ramaswamy, Venkat (2004) *The Future of Competition: Co-creating unique value with customers*, Harvard Business School Press, Boston, MA

Ridderstråle, Jonas and Nordström, Kjell (2004a) *Funky Business*, Financial Times Prentice Hall, London

Ridderstråle, Jonas and Nordström, Kjell (2004b) *Karaoke Capitalism: Managing for mankind*, Financial Times Prentice Hall, London

Simon, Hermann (1996) *Hidden Champions: Lessons from 500 of the world's best unknown companies*, Harvard Business School Press, Boston, MA

Journals

Absatzwirtschaft – www.absatzwirtschaft.de

Acquisa – www.acquisa.de

brand eins – www.brandeins.de

Business Bestseller – www.business-bestseller.com

Capital – www.capital.de

Fast Company – www.fastcompany.com

Harvard Business Manager – www.harvardbusinessmanager.de

Impulse – www.impulse.de

Marketing & Kommunikation – www.m-k.ch

Persönlich – www.persoenlich.com

Trendletter – www.trendletter.de

Index

NB: page numbers in *italic* indicate figures, illustrations or tables